UK AIRFRYER RECIPE BOOK 2024

Air Fryer Meals for Your Whole Family and Busy People on a Budget

Copyright©2023 Sophie Gill

All rights reserved. No part of this book may be reproduced or used in any manner without the prior written permission of the copyright owner, except for the use of brief quotations in a book review.

Printed by Amazon in the USA.

Disclaimer : Although the author and publisher have made every effort to ensure that the information in this book was correct at press time, the author and publisher do not assume and hereby disclaim any liability to any party for any loss, damage, or disruption caused by errors or omissions, whether such errors or omissions result from negligence, accident, or any other cause. this book is not intended as a substitute for the medical advice of physicians.

CONTENTS

INTRODUCTION 5

AIR FRYER RECIPES 9

How To Make Ham And Cheese Toastie In Air Fryer 10
How To Cook Baked Potato In An Air Fryer 11
How To Cook Frozen Breaded Fish In An Air Fryer 12
How To Cook Fillet Steak In An Air Fryer 13
How To Make French Toast In An Air Fryer 14
How To Make Chicken Kievs In An Air Fryer 15
How To Make Bread In An Air Fryer 16
How To Make Poached Eggs In An Air Fryer 17
Air Fryer Chicken Thighs Recipe 18
Air Fryer Cheese Toastie Recipe 19
How To Cook Lamb Chops In An Air Fryer 20
How To Make Sweet Potato Fries In An Air Fryer .. 21
How To Make Home Made Chips In Air Fryer 22
How To Cook Frozen Tempura Prawns In Air Fryer 23
How To Cook Frozen Onion Rings In An Air Fryer . 24
How To Cook Frozen Curly Fries In An Air Fryer ... 25
How To Cook Frozen Mozzarella Sticks In Air Fryer 26
How To Cook Fish Fingers In An Air Fryer 27
How To Cook Frozen Pizza In Air Fryer 28
How To Cook Frozen Meatballs In Air Fryer 29
How To Cook Frozen Burgers In An Air Fryer 30
How To Cook Frozen Hash Browns In Air Fryer..... 31
How To Make Jacket Potato In Air Fryer 32
How To Cook Roast Potatoes In An Air Fryer 33
How To Cook Steak In An Air Fryer........................ 34
How To Cook Frozen Broccoli In Air Fryer 35

How To Cook Broccoli In Air Fryer 36
How To Cook Fried Chicken In An Air Fryer 37
How To Cook Buffalo Wings In An Air Fryer 38
How To Cook Chips In An Air Fryer 39
How To Cook Chicken Breast In An Air Fryer 40
How To Cook Potato Wedges In An Air Fryer 41
How To Cook Burgers In An Air Fryer.................... 42
How To Cook Onion Rings In An Air Fryer 43
How To Cook Hash Browns In An Air Fryer........... 44
How To Cook Chicken Nuggets In An Air Fryer 45
How To Cook Salmon In An Air Fryer 46
How To Make Chocolate Brownies In An Air Fryer 47
How To Cook Frozen Samosa In An Air Fryer........ 48
How To Cook Meatballs In An Air Fryer 49
How To Cook Chicken Wings In An Air Fryer 50
Chicken And Bacon Burger 51
Fried Chicken Sandwich... 52
Pork Chops With Sloe Sauce And Savoy Cabbage ... 53
Fish And Chips With Tartare Sauce 54
How To Make Fish Pie.. 55
Roast Pork And Veg With Gravy 56
Banana Chips.. 57
Air Fryer Roast Chicken 58
Air Fryer Crispy Chicken Burger............................. 59
Air Fryer Chicken Wings With Honey And Sesame 60
Air Fryer Fish And Chips With Tartare Sauce 61
Air Fryer Spicy Pork Belly 62
Air Fryer Chicken Parmigiana................................. 63
Air Fryer Falafel... 64

3

Air Fryer Chips	65
Air Fryer Chicken Fajitas	66
Air Fryer Easy Crispy Chilli Beef	67
Air Fryer Chicken Strips	68
Air Fryer Meatballs With Cherry Tomato Sauce	69
Air Fryer Beef Tacos	70
Air Fryer Sausage Rolls With Black Pudding	71
Air Fryer Pork Chops	72
Air Fryer Mozzarella Sticks	73
Air Fryer Blueberry Baked Oats	74
Air Fryer Baked Eggs	75
Air Fryer Chicken Thighs With Honey, Chilli And Soy Glaze	76
Air Fryer Sausage Bake	77
Air Fryer Salmon With Warm Potato Salad	78
Air Fryer Crispy Tofu	79
Air Fryer Beef Tacos	80
Air Fryer Pork Steak Sandwich	81
Air Fryer Tomato, Pepper And Feta Pasta	82
Air Fryer Sweet Potato And Chorizo Hash	83
Air Fryer Pizza	84
Air Fryer Sweet Potato Fries	85
Air Fryer Roast Potatoes	86
Air Fryer Sausage And Bean Casserole	87
Air Fryer Baked Potato	88
Air Fryer Cauliflower 'Wings'	89
Air Fryer Chipotle Peppers And Gnocchi	90
Salmon With Roasted Miso Vegetables	91
Air Fryer Gnocchi With Pesto Dip	92
Air Fryer Tofu Nuggets	93
Air Fryer Roast Sprouts	94
Mini Hasselback Potatoes	95
Teriyaki Root Vegetable Salad With Crispy Tofu	96
Baked Vegetable Crisps	97
Curried Pumpkin Soup	98
Vietnamese-Style Loaded Fries	99
Easy Onion Rings	100
Air Fryer Yoghurt Custard Toast	101
Air Fryer Apple-Topped Cake	102
4-Ingredient Air Fryer Cookies	103
Air Fryer Courgette, Almond And Pine Nut Cake	104
Air Fryer Peach Turnovers	105
Roasted Pumpkin Seeds	106
Air Fryer Apple, Pear And Raspberry Crumble	107
Homemade Granola	108

INTRODUCTION

The best air fryer models are increasingly becoming a go to in UK households. With energy bills soaring and an air fryer's operating costs relatively low, they have become a great alternative to the oven or deep frying. Air fryers can also be healthier than other options and are famous for their ability to replicate deep fried foods with far less oil, using air as the vehicle for heat.

Busy parents are often keen for ways to shave precious time off their daily routines, whether that's using a slow cooker for efficient, effortless food prep, or using a gadget like an air fryer to actually reduce the overall cooking time needed for meals. We're certainly all on board with anything that makes family life easier, and Mumsnet users rave about the time and money-saving qualities of an air fryer. Using your air fryer can extend to cooking a wide range of dishes from pizza and chips for dinner, to fried eggs and bacon for breakfast. Whether you're a total beginner or have been using an air fryer for some time, our guide has loads of tips, tricks and dinner inspiration to get your mouth watering...

HOW AIR FRYERS WORK

Air fryers work by circulating hot air around food. Inside, the air fryer will have a heating element which warms up the air, passing it over and around the food in the cooking chamber. This is what creates the trademark crispy effect people love so much about air-fried food. And you don't have to add much oil too. Reducing the amount of oil you use in your cooking is one of the key benefits of using air fryers: they allow for healthier cooking. Air fryers require little oil in comparison to other cooking methods, lowering the amount of unhealthy fat in your food. This small change can improve your heart health and lower your cholesterol. Additionally, not submerging your foods in oil preserves their nutritional value better.

Another benefit of using an air fryer is that they reduce cooking time. They preheat quickly, and cook food evenly and rapidly, reducing cooking time by up to 30% compared to oven baking. This makes home cooking much easier; you can get delicious food on the table rapidly, and focus on the important stuff like quality family time.

The size of air fryers in relation to conventional ovens makes one of their advantages their convenience too, although bear in mind that you will need to make space on your countertop. They are usually easy to clean, with most containing dishwasher-safe parts. All in all, they are an appliance ideal for people with busy lives, including parents and those struggling to find time in the kitchen after a long day at work.

DO YOU PUT OIL IN AN AIR FRYER?

Don't let the name deceive you, you still do need to use oil in your air fryer as it plays an important role in the cooking process. Air fryers typically require around a teaspoon or two per dish. It's still much less than what you'd use for oven cooking or in a deep fat fryer. Just make sure you put the oil directly onto the food, and give it a good shake regularly for an even satisfying crisp.

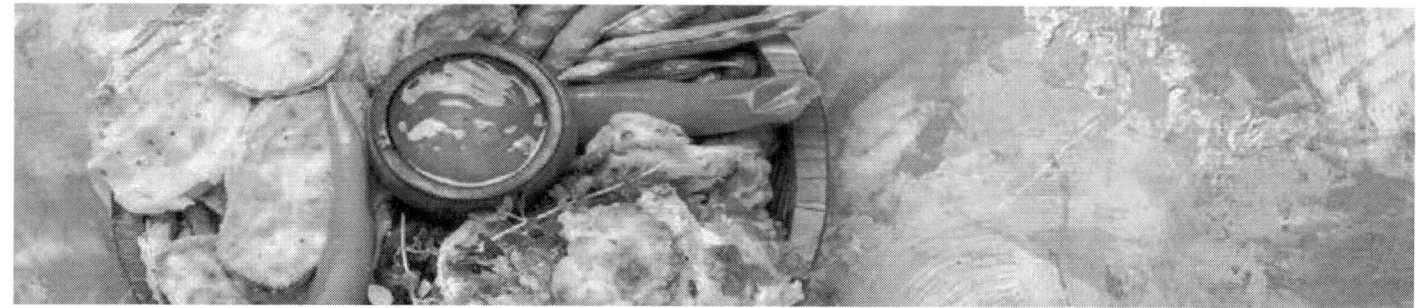

AIR FRYER TIPS FOR BEGINNERS: WHAT TO KNOW BEFORE YOUR FIRST USE

Never air-fried before? Here are some insider tips to get you started with a basket-style air fryer:

1. Preheat: Remember to preheat your air fryer before putting the food in. It should heat up much faster than a standard oven.
2. Add a slice of bread: A well-placed slice of bread in the bottom of your air fryer can be helpful for collecting any excess grease, making the post-meal clean up easier.
3. Spray with oil during the cooking process: This helps to ensure a nice even crisp. However, you don't need to do this for greasy meats like bacon or sausages.
4. Move food around: Shaking the basket a little during the cooking process helps to ensure everything is cooked evenly.
5. Use in a well ventilated space: Leave plenty of space around the air fryer for ventilation. Do not use right next to a wall.

HOW TO USE YOUR AIR FRYER

Here's a handy step-by-step guide to cooking food with a basket air fryer. How to use it will differ from meal to meal and between models (it will be slightly different for air fryer ovens too), so you should always consult the instructions before starting, but these are generally the steps involved in air frying.

1. Prepare your ingredients: Cut the food items down to uniform size so they cook evenly.
2. Preheat the air fryer and select the program you want to use: It's important to let your air fryer reach its designated temperature and let it preheat for about five minutes before you put the food in.
3. Add the food: Add the food in an even layer in the fry basket, leaving some space to allow hot air to circulate.
4. Cook: Place the fry basket in the air fryer and set the cooking time. Cooking times vary depending on the type of food so you should always check this, but a general rule of thumb is to cook for 10 to 15 minutes, shaking the tray and flipping the food halfway through.
5. Check: Open the air fryer and check the food. If it's not done to your liking, continue cooking in five-minute increments until it is cooked.
6. Serve: Use oven mitts to remove the fry basket from the air fryer and serve.

MISTAKES TO AVOID

- Not preheating: Like with any cooking appliance, heating your air fryer before you add food means it will cook as soon as it's put inside. If you put your food inside as the fryer is heating up, it will get soggy.
- Overfilling the basket: Because air fryers use hot air to cook, you need to leave space between the items to allow air flow and encourage even cooking.
- Using foods that don't weigh enough: It may sound silly, but when using circulating air to cook food, you need to ensure what's inside weighs enough that the fan won't blow it around. Things like kale and bread might be too light to cook in your air fryer.
- Go easy on the oil: Too much oil can result in overly greasy food and may cause the air fryer to get too smoke, so go easy on the oil, particularly if the food you're cooking is already quite fatty.
- Not cleaning properly after use: Cleaning your air fryer thoroughly will help you preserve its life. If you don't clean it, food can build up in the basket and become difficult to remove.

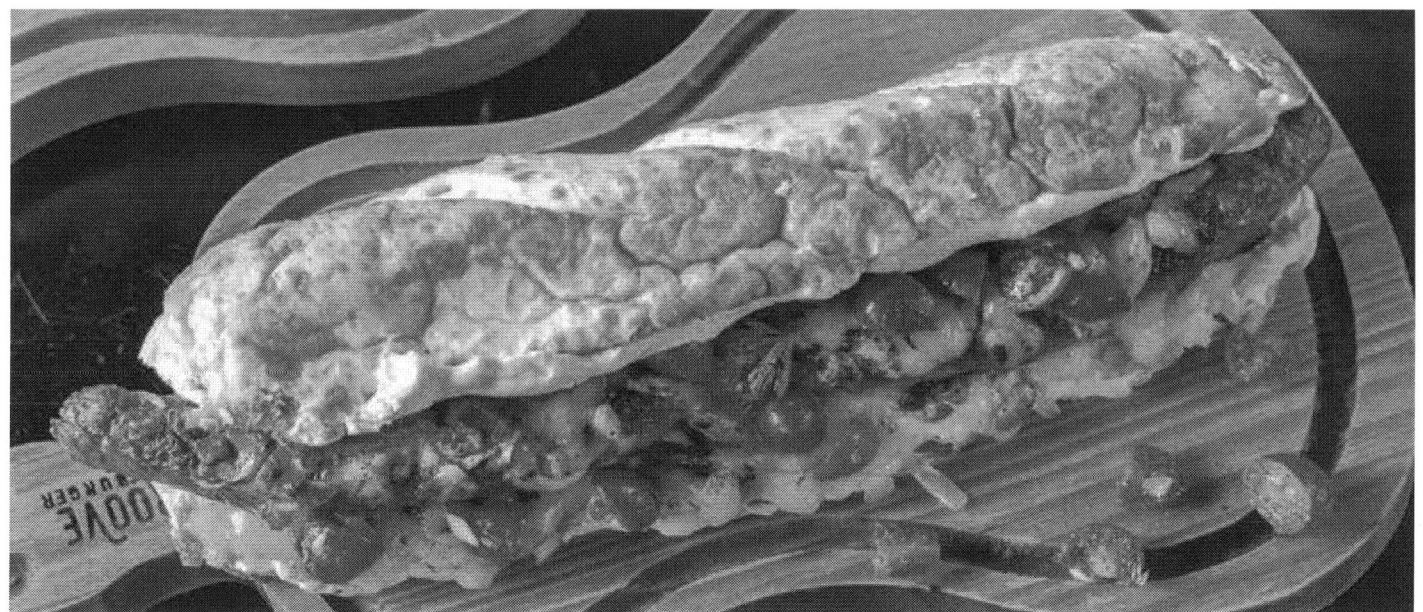

THE BEST FOODS TO COOK IN AN AIR FRYER

Here are just some of the delicious treats Mumsnet users recommend air frying:

- Chips: If any food is synonymous with air frying, it's crispy chips.
- All potato-based products (apart from mash): Your air fryer will easily outperform your oven on crispiness and cooking speed.
- Chicken wings: Crispy skin and much healthier than deep frying... what's not to like?
- Vegetables: From carrots to brussell sprouts, vegetables cook quickly and evenly in an air fryer. The high heat caramelises the natural sugars in the vegetables, creating a delicious flavour.
- Fish: The even heat of the air fryer creates the perfect flaky texture for your fish fillets.
- Bacon: Crispy bacon is an air fryer speciality. Learn how to use your air fryer to get the crispiest bacon and don't look back...
- Sweet treats: Air fryers are great for more than just savoury food. Try cakes and muffins for delicious results.
- Reheated food: Air fryers are fantastic for reheating food. They won't make once-crispy things mushy like a microwave will. Use them to revive leftovers or last night's takeaway!

HOW TO CLEAN YOUR AIR FRYER

Knowing how to use an air fryer also involves knowing how to take care of it. To keep it functioning well you should regularly clean it. First, unplug it and allow it to cool down. Then empty out any remaining food and crumbs from the fry basket and wipe it down with a damp cloth. For stuck-on food or grease, fill the basket with warm soapy water and let it soak for 10-15 minutes before scrubbing it with a sponge or brush. If there are any stubborn spots, try using a mixture of baking soda and water to scrub away.

Next, clean the interior. Use a damp cloth to wipe down the interior and remove any grease or food particles. For more thorough cleaning, you can remove the tray and wash it in the dishwasher (if it is dishwasher safe) or by hand. If there are any hard-to-reach areas, use a cotton swab or toothbrush to clean them.

Finally, be sure to regularly clean the outside. Use a damp cloth to wipe down the outside and remove any smudges. Regular cleaning will keep your air fryer in good working condition and prevent any build-up of grease or grime that could negatively affect the taste of your food.

AIR FRYER RECIPES

How To Make Ham And Cheese Toastie In Air Fryer

Ingredients:
- 4 slices of bread
- 2 slices of ham
- 2 slices of cheese
- Butter

Directions:
1. Preheat your air fryer to 180°C or 350°F.
2. Butter one side of each slice of bread.
3. On the non-buttered side of two slices, place a slice of cheese and ham.
4. Place the remaining slices of bread on top, buttered side up.
5. Place the sandwiches into the air fryer.
6. Cook for 5 minutes, then flip the sandwiches over.
7. Continue cooking for another 3-5 minutes or until the bread is toasted to your liking and the cheese has melted.

Notes:
1. Bread selection: Opt for a sturdy type of bread like sourdough or a thick whole grain. Thinly sliced bread may not hold up as well in the air fryer.
2. Cheese choices: While Cheddar and Swiss are classic choices, feel free to experiment with other types like Gouda, Provolone or Pepper Jack.
3. Ham alternatives: If you want to switch it up, try using turkey, roast beef, or even cooked bacon.
4. Butter or no butter: If you prefer a healthier option, you can skip the butter and just use cooking spray on the bread.
5. Serving suggestions: Pair your ham and cheese toasties with a side of chips, fruits, or even a small salad for a more filling meal. You can also add some sliced tomatoes, avocado, or pesto to elevate the flavour.
6. Storage and reheating: If you want to save some for later, let the toasties cool completely before storing them in an airtight container in the fridge. To reheat, pop them back into the air fryer for a few minutes until heated through.

How To Cook Baked Potato In An Air Fryer

Ingredients:
- 4 medium-sized Russet potatoes
- Olive oil
- Salt and pepper to taste
- Your preferred toppings such as sour cream, cheddar cheese, and chives

Directions:
1. Start by washing and drying the potatoes.
2. Rub olive oil all over the potatoes.
3. Sprinkle them with salt and pepper.
4. Place the potatoes in the air fryer basket, leaving enough space between each one.
5. Set the temperature to 200°C (400°F) and cook for 20-25 minutes, or until they're crispy on the outside and soft inside.
6. Once done, carefully remove the potatoes from the air fryer (they will be hot!).
7. Slice them open, fluff the insides with a fork, and add your favourite toppings.

How To Cook Frozen Breaded Fish In An Air Fryer

Ingredients:
- Frozen breaded fish fillets

Directions:
1. Preheat your air fryer to 200°C or 390°F.
2. Arrange the frozen breaded fish fillets in the air fryer basket.
3. Cook the fish fillets for 7 minutes at 200°C.
4. After 7 minutes, remove the fry basket and flip the fish.
5. Cook again for another 7 minutes at 200 °C.
6. Check if the fish is thoroughly cooked by ensuring it's flaky and has reached an internal temperature of 70°C.

Notes:
1. Here are some tips and considerations when cooking frozen breaded fish in an air fryer:
2. Do not thaw the fish before air frying. The beauty of using an air fryer is that you can cook frozen food directly.
3. Depending on the thickness of your fish fillets, you may need to adjust the cooking time. Thicker fillets will require more time while thinner ones will cook faster.
4. If you want a crispy and golden exterior, lightly spray the fish with olive oil before air frying.
5. Avoid overcrowding the air fryer basket. This will result in uneven cooking.
6. Always use a thermometer to check the internal temperature of the fish to ensure it's fully cooked.

How To Cook Fillet Steak In An Air Fryer

Ingredients:
- 2 fillet steaks
- Salt to taste
- Freshly ground black pepper
- Olive oil
- Garlic powder
- Onion powder

Directions:
1. Preheat your air fryer to 200°C (400°F).
2. Season your steaks with salt, black pepper, garlic powder, onion powder, and a drizzle of olive oil.
3. Once preheated, place the seasoned steaks in the air fryer basket.
4. Cook for 8-10 minutes for medium-rare or 13-18 minutes for medium to well-done.
5. Let the steak rest for a few minutes before serving.

How To Make French Toast In An Air Fryer

Ingredients:
- 4 slices of bread
- 1/2 cup of milk
- 1 teaspoon of vanilla extract
- 1/2 teaspoon of cinnamon
- 2 large eggs
- 1/4 cup of granulated sugar
- Maple syrup and powdered sugar for topping

Directions:
1. In a shallow dish, whisk together the eggs, milk, vanilla extract, cinnamon, and sugar.
2. Dip each slice of bread into the egg mixture, ensuring both sides are well-coated.
3. Arrange the soaked bread slices in a single layer in your air fryer basket. Do not overcrowd.
4. Set the air fryer to 185°C and cook for 8 minutes, flipping the slices halfway through the cooking time.
5. Once golden brown, remove the French toast from the air fryer and drizzle with maple syrup and a dusting of powdered sugar.

Notes:
1. Ensure your bread slices are thick enough to hold up in the air fryer.
2. Don't skip flipping your French toast halfway through the cooking time. It ensures even browning and crispiness.
3. Remember, air fryer models can vary in power. Keep an eye on your French toast to prevent burning.

How To Make Chicken Kievs In An Air Fryer

Ingredients:
- 4 skinless chicken breasts
- 4 tablespoons of butter
- 2 cloves of garlic, minced
- 2 tablespoons of fresh parsley, chopped
- 1 cup of flour
- 3 eggs, beaten
- 2 cups of breadcrumbs
- Salt and pepper to season
- Cooking spray

Directions:
1. Begin by making the garlic butter. Mix the butter, minced garlic, and chopped parsley together in a bowl. Divide into four and shape into small logs. Freeze until solid.
2. Flatten the chicken breasts using a meat mallet or rolling pin. Place a log of garlic butter in the center of each breast, fold in the sides and roll up tightly. Secure with toothpicks if necessary.
3. Set up three separate bowls with the flour, beaten eggs, and breadcrumbs. Season the chicken with salt and pepper, then dip each rolled chicken breast first in the flour, then the egg, and finally the breadcrumbs.
4. Preheat your air fryer to 180°C (350°F). Spray the breadcrumb-coated chicken with cooking spray and place them in the air fryer basket.
5. Cook the chicken for 20-25 minutes, or until golden brown and cooked through. Let them rest for a few minutes before serving.

How To Make Bread In An Air Fryer

Ingredients:
- 1 cup of warm water
- 2 teaspoons of active dry yeast
- 1 teaspoon of sugar
- 3 cups of all-purpose flour
- 1 teaspoon of salt
- 1 tablespoon of olive oil

Directions:
1. In a small bowl, mix the warm water, sugar, and yeast. Let it sit for about 5 minutes until it becomes frothy.
2. Mix the salt and flour in another large bowl, then make a well in the middle and pour in the yeast mixture (from step 1) and the olive oil.
3. Stir the mixture until it forms a dough. Knead the dough on a lightly floured surface for about 10 minutes until it becomes smooth and elastic.
4. Place the dough in a greased bowl, cover it with a towel, and let it rise in a warm place for about 1 hour, or until it has doubled in size.
5. Preheat your air fryer to 180°C (350°F). Place the dough in the air fryer basket and cook for about 15 minutes, or until the bread is golden brown and sounds hollow when tapped.
6. Allow the bread to cool before slicing.

Notes:
1. Making bread in an air fryer is generally straightforward, but here are some tips and considerations to keep in mind:
2. Yeast activation: Make sure your yeast is activated before adding it to the dough. It should foam up when mixed with warm water and sugar.
3. Dough consistency: The dough should be soft and slightly sticky, but not overly wet.
4. Air fryer capacity: Ensure your air fryer is large enough to accommodate the rising dough.
5. Temperature and time: Every air fryer is different. Monitor the bread closely the first time you make it to determine the best cooking time and temperature.

How To Make Poached Eggs In An Air Fryer

Ingredients:
- 2-4 eggs
- Boiling water (from a kettle)
- Salt
- Pepper
- Cooking spray
- Small heatproof bowls or ramekins

Directions:
1. Preheat your air fryer to 200°C.
2. Lightly spray your small bowls or ramekins with cooking spray.
3. Fill them about halfway way with boiling water.
4. Crack an egg into each bowl or ramekin.
5. Place the bowls or ramekins into the air fryer basket.
6. Cook at 200°C for 6 minutes, or until the egg whites are set but the yolks are still runny.
7. Carefully remove the bowls or ramekins from the air fryer (they will be hot!), pour out the water, and season the poached eggs with salt and pepper.

Air Fryer Chicken Thighs Recipe

Ingredients:
- 4 bone-in, skin-on chicken thighs
- 1 tablespoon olive oil
- Salt and pepper to taste
- 1 teaspoon garlic powder
- 1 teaspoon onion powder
- 1/2 teaspoon paprika
- Fresh herbs for garnish (optional)

Directions:
1. Preheat your air fryer to 200°C (400°F).
2. Rinse the chicken thighs and pat them dry with a paper towel.
3. In a bowl, mix together the olive oil, salt, pepper, garlic powder, onion powder, and paprika.
4. Rub the mixture all over the chicken thighs, ensuring they are well coated.
5. Place the chicken thighs in the air fryer basket, skin side up. Ensure they are not touching.
6. Cook for 25-30 minutes or until the chicken thighs reach an internal temperature of 74°C (165°F)
7. Let the chicken rest for a few minutes before serving.

Air Fryer Cheese Toastie Recipe

Ingredients:
- 4 slices of bread (white or brown as per preference)
- 2 cups of grated cheddar cheese
- 2 tablespoons of butter, softened
- Optional: add-ins like sliced tomatoes, cooked bacon, or caramelized onions

Directions:
1. Preheat your air fryer to 200°C (or 390°F).
2. While the air fryer is heating up, spread a thin layer of butter on one side of each slice of bread.
3. Place half of the grated cheese on the unbuttered side of two slices.
4. Add your optional ingredients, if any, on top of the cheese.
5. Cover with the remaining cheese and top with the remaining slices of bread, buttered side up.
6. Once the air fryer is preheated, place the sandwiches in the basket, making sure not to overcrowd it.
7. Cook for 5-7 minutes, or until the bread is golden brown and the cheese has melted.
8. Carefully remove the hot sandwiches from the air fryer and let them cool for a minute before cutting into halves and serving.

Notes:
1. Choice of Cheese: Cheddar is a classic choice, but you can experiment with different types of cheese like mozzarella, gouda, or a combination of your favourites.
2. Bread Selection: While white bread is traditional for toasties, feel free to try with whole grain, sourdough, or even gluten-free bread.
3. Avoid Overfilling: Don't add too much cheese or fillings, as it might leak out and cause a mess in your air fryer.
4. Rotate the Sandwiches: If you're making more than one sandwich, rotate them halfway through cooking for even browning.

How To Cook Lamb Chops In An Air Fryer

Ingredients:
- Lamb chops: 4 pieces
- Olive oil: 2 tablespoons
- Garlic: 2 cloves, minced
- Rosemary: 1 tablespoon, chopped
- Thyme: 1 tablespoon, chopped
- Salt: 1 teaspoon
- Black pepper: 1/2 teaspoon

Directions:
1. To marinate the lamb chops, combine all the ingredients in a large bowl and mix well.
2. Add the lamb chops to the bowl and toss to coat them evenly with the marinade.
3. Cover the bowl with plastic wrap and refrigerate for at least 1 hour or up to overnight.
4. The longer you marinate the lamb chops, the more flavourful they will be. However, be careful not to over-marinate them as the acid in the marinade can break down the meat and make it mushy.
5. Once the lamb chops are marinated, remove them from the refrigerator and let them sit at room temperature for 10-15 minutes before cooking. This will allow the meat to cook evenly and prevent it from becoming tough.

How To Make Sweet Potato Fries In An Air Fryer

Ingredients:
- 2 large sweet potatoes, cut into 1/4-inch sticks
- 1 tablespoon olive oil
- Salt and pepper to taste

Directions:
1. Peel, wash, and cut your sweet potatoes.
2. Place the sweet potato fries in a bowl and drizzle with olive oil. Sprinkle with salt and pepper then toss to coat evenly.
3. Place the sweet potato fries in an even layer in the air fryer basket without having them overlap each other.
4. Set your air fryer timer to 8 minutes and the temperature to 200°C and let it cook.
5. After 8 minutes, remove the fry basket and shake it around a few times to ensure even cooking.
6. Replace the fry basket and cook again for another 7 minutes.
7. Check and see if the fries are cooked to your liking, if you want it crispier, add 3-5 minutes more.

Notes:
1. Make sure you cut the sweet potatoes into even pieces so they can cook evenly.
2. Make sure you stop the fryer and shake the basket to ensure even cooking. Don't skip this step, it really does help.
3. If your air fryer has a variable temperature setting, you can adjust it to get the desired crispiness.

How To Make Home Made Chips In Air Fryer

Ingredients:
- 2-4 potatoes, depending on how many people you're cooking for
- Cooking spray or olive oil
- Salt and pepper (optional)
- Paper towel

Directions:
1. Wash and scrub your potatoes. You can also peel them if you like, or you can leave the skin on if you prefer it like that.
2. Cut your potatoes into thin slices if you want thin-cut chips (1cm should be fine), or cut them a bit thicker if you want thick-cut chips.
3. Soak the slices in a bowl of cold water for at least 15 minutes, this will help to get rid of some of the starch and give the chips a crispier texture after frying.
4. After 15 minutes, drain the potato slices and pat dry them with a paper towel.
5. Add a few squirts of cooking spray to your air fryer basket.
6. Spread a sing layer of chips into the fry basket, do not stack them or overcrowd the basket. Cook multiple batches instead of stacking.
7. (Optional) Spray with olive oil, then sprinkle with salt and pepper or any other seasonings of your choice if you want.
8. Set your air fryer temperature to 190°C/380°F and the timer to 7 minutes and let it cook.
9. After 7 minutes, remove the fry basket and give it a good shake, this will help to ensure even cooking.
10. Replace the fry basket again and cook for another 7 minutes.
11. Remove the fry basket again and give it another shake.
12. Replace the fry basket and cook for the final 7 minutes. If you're doing thick-cut chips, increase this to 9 minutes.
13. Check on the chips and see if they're crispy enough for your liking, if not, add an extra 2-4 minutes and cook again.

How To Cook Frozen Tempura Prawns In Air Fryer

Ingredients:
- Frozen tempura prawns
- Cooking spray

Directions:
1. Add a few sprays of cooking spray to your air fryer basket.
2. Place as many of the frozen tempura prawns as you can fit in the fry basket without stacking them or creating an overlap. Cook in batches if needed.
3. Set your air fryer temperature to 200°C/400°F and the timer to 4 minutes and let the tempura prawns cook.
4. After 4 minutes, remove the fry basket and flip the prawns over.
5. Replace the fry basket and cook for another 4 minutes.
6. Remove the fry basket and check if the tempura prawns are golden brown. If it is, that's it. Done. If not, add an extra 1-2 minutes.

How To Cook Frozen Onion Rings In An Air Fryer

Ingredients:
- Frozen onion rings
- Cooking spray

Directions:
1. Add a few sprays of cooking spray to the bottom of your air fryer basket.
2. Add a single layer of frozen onion rings to your air fryer basket. Stacking will cause some of the onion rings to cook unevenly, instead, cook multiple batches if needed.
3. Set your air fryer temperature to 400°F/200°C and cook for 4 minutes.
4. After 4 minutes, remove the fry basket and shake it around a couple of times, if you're cooking large onion rings, use tongs and flip them over, this will help to promote even cooking, and it will help stop the onion rings from sticking to the fry basket.
5. Replace the fry basket and cook for another 4 minutes at the same temperature.

How To Cook Frozen Curly Fries In An Air Fryer

Ingredients:
- 1/2 bag of seasoned or plain curly fries
- Cooking spray

Directions:
1. Select the pre-heat function on your air fryer and let it run its course, if your air fryer does not have a pre-heat function, set the air fryer to 400°F/200°C and let it run for 2 minutes.
2. After preheating, remove the fry basket and add a few sprays of cooking spray, make sure you cover the entire base of the fry basket.
3. Add the frozen curly fries to the fry basket, a little stacking is ok but try to avoid over-stacking them, the fries will shrink while cooking, so a little bit of stacking is fine.
4. Set your air fryer to 400°F/200°C and cook the curly fries for 5 minutes.
5. After 5 minutes, remove the fry basket and give it a good shake to make sure all the fries cook evenly.
6. Replace the fry basket and cook again for another 4-5 minutes at the same temperature.

How To Cook Frozen Mozzarella Sticks In Air Fryer

Ingredients:
- 1 pack of frozen mozzarella sticks
- Cooking spray
- Your favourite dipping sauce (optional)

Directions:
1. Add a few sprays of cooking spray to the fry basket.
2. Place the frozen mozzarella sticks in the air fryer basket, do not let them overlap, cook in batches if necessary.
3. Set your air fryer to 200°C/400°F and cook for 6 minutes.
4. Serve with your favourite dipping sauce and enjoy!

How To Cook Fish Fingers In An Air Fryer

Ingredients:

- 10-12 Fish fingers per batch (depending on the size of your air fryer)
- Cooking spray

Directions:

1. Add a few sprays of cooking spray to the fry basket.
2. Add a single layer of fish fingers to the fry basket. Do not stack or allow the fish fingers to overlap each other, this will cause some of the fish fingers to be soggy and undercooked.
3. Set your air fryer temperature to 400°F/200°C and cook for 9 minutes.
4. After 9 minutes, remove the fry basket and check if the fish fingers are crispy enough for your liking. If not, add an extra 2 minutes and cook again.

How To Cook Frozen Pizza In Air Fryer

Ingredients:
- Cooking spray (optional)
- Frozen Pizza

Directions:
1. Add a few sprays of cooking spray to the air fryer basket. (optional)
2. Add the frozen pizza to your air fryer basket.
3. Set the air fryer timer to 8 minutes and the temperature to 400°F/200°C and let the pizza cook.
4. If your pizza has toppings e.g pepperoni, remove the fry basket after 4 minutes and check if these toppings have blown off, this sometimes happens because air fryers use rapid hot air to cook food.
5. Replace the fry basket and cook for the remaining 4 minutes.

How To Cook Frozen Meatballs In Air Fryer

Ingredients:
- Cooking spray
- Frozen Meatballs

Directions:
1. Add a light coat of cooking spray to your air fryer basket.
2. Spread a single layer of frozen meatballs in the fry basket. Be sure not to overcrowd the basket, as this will prevent the meatballs from cooking evenly. If necessary, cook them in batches.
3. Set the air fryer temperature to 200°C/190°F and the timer to 6 minutes and let it cook.
4. After 6 minutes, remove the fry basket and give it a good shake to ensure all the meatballs cook evenly.
5. Replace the fry basket and cook for another 6 minutes.
6. Serve with your favourite dipping sauce and enjoy!

How To Cook Frozen Burgers In An Air Fryer

Ingredients:

- Cooking spray
- 1-2 Frozen burger patties
- Cheese (optional)
- Lettuce, onions, pickles, etc. (Optional)

Directions:

1. Spray the bottom of your fry basket with some cooking spray or olive oil.
2. Add 1-2 frozen burger patties to the fry basket. Do not let them overlap each other. Just a little space between them is fine, the burgers will shrink while cooking.
3. Set the temperature to 400°F/200°C and the air fryer timer to 13 minutes and let the burgers cook.
4. After 6 minutes, remove the fry basket and flip the burgers over.
5. Replace the fry basket and let the burgers cook for the remaining 7 minutes.
6. After cooking for 13 minutes, open the fry basket and top your burger with a slice of cheese, replace the fry basket and let it sit for 1 minute. (Optional)
7. Remove the burgers from the air fryer and add your lettuce, onions, pickles, etc. Enjoy! (Optional)

How To Cook Frozen Hash Browns In Air Fryer

Ingredients:
- Cooking spray/olive oil
- Frozen hash browns

Directions:
1. Spray the bottom of your air fryer basket with cooking spray/olive oil.
2. Lay a single layer of hash browns in the fry basket. Do not stack.
3. Cook for 5 minutes at 200°C/400°F.
4. After 5 minutes, remove the fry basket and flip the hash browns.
5. Replace the fry basket and cook for another 6 minutes.
6. Check and ensure they're crispy enough for your liking, if not, cook for another 1-2 minutes.

How To Make Jacket Potato In Air Fryer

Ingredients:
- 1 Large baking potato
- 1/2 Tablespoon olive oil
- Salt and pepper
- Optional toppings: butter, cheese, beans, tuna, etc.

Directions:
1. Preheat your air fryer to 200°C/400°F.
2. While the air fryer is warming up, wash your potato and slice it in half lengthwise.
3. Rub the potato halves with olive oil and season with salt and pepper.
4. Place the potato halves in the air fryer basket and cook at 200°C/400°F for 20 minutes.
5. Remove from the air fryer and add your desired toppings. Serve immediately. Enjoy!

Notes:
1. Experiment with different types of potatoes: While Russet potatoes are the go-to choice for jacket potatoes, don't be afraid to try other varieties such as Yukon Gold or sweet potatoes. Each type will bring a unique flavour and texture to your dish.
2. Don't overcrowd your air fryer: Make sure there is enough space between each potato in the air fryer basket for proper airflow. Overcrowding can result in unevenly cooked potatoes.
3. Season well: Rub a little bit of oil (olive oil or vegetable oil works well) all over the potato and then season generously with salt. This step not only adds flavour but also gives the potato its characteristic crispy skin.
4. Experiment with different toppings and fillings: While traditional jacket potatoes are usually topped with butter, cheese and sour cream, don't be afraid to experiment with other toppings and fillings such as bacon, chilli or even pulled pork.

How To Cook Roast Potatoes In An Air Fryer

Ingredients:
- 2-4 Large Potatoes (Depending on how many people)
- 1 Teaspoon Paprika
- 1 Teaspoon Italian Seasoning
- 1/2 Teaspoon Red Pepper Flakes
- 1 Teaspoon Onion Powder
- 1 Teaspoon Garlic Granules
- 1 Tablespoon Olive Oil

Directions:
1. Wash and scrub the potatoes to get rid of any dirt.
2. Cut the potatoes into smaller pieces, you don't have to peel them, try to keep the slices the same thickness to ensure they cook evenly.
3. Place the cut potatoes in a bowl. Add the paprika, Italian seasoning, pepper flakes, onion powder, garlic granules add lastly the olive oil. Toss all the ingredients around until all the potatoes are evenly coated.
4. Add a few sprays of olive oil to the fry basket to ensure the potatoes don't stick, then place the potatoes into the fryer basket.
5. Cook at 200°C/400°F for 10 minutes.
6. Remove the fry basket and give it a good shake or flip the potatoes with a fork or tongs, you can add a few sprays of cooking oil here again if you want.
7. Replace the basket and cook again at 200°C/400°F for 10-15 minutes, keep checking between 10-15 minutes to see when they're crispy and golden.

How To Cook Steak In An Air Fryer

Ingredients:
- 2 Cuts of Steak
- Salt and Pepper
- 2 Tablespoons Butter (room temperature)
- ½ Tablespoon Freshly Chopped Parsley
- ½ Teaspoon Minced Garlic
- ¼ Teaspoon Worcestershire Sauce

Directions:
1. Preheat your air fryer at 200°C/400°F for 3 minutes.
2. While the air fryer is preheating, mix the butter, chopped parsley, minced garlic and Worcestershire sauce in a small bowl.
3. Season the steaks with salt and pepper then place them in the air fryer basket. Ensure there's enough room between them for the hot air to circulate. If the steaks are too big, do them one at a time instead of stacking.
4. Cook at 200°C/400°F for 6 minutes.
5. After 6 minutes, open the fry basket and flip and rotate the steaks. This will allow the steaks to cook evenly.
6. Replace the fry basket and cook for another 6 minutes. If you prefer them well done, cook for 8 minutes instead.
7. Remove the fry basket and let the steaks sit for roughly 6 minutes. Again, this will help to promote even cooking.
8. Add the garlic butter sauce and spread it out with a spoon. Enjoy!

How To Cook Frozen Broccoli In Air Fryer

Ingredients:
- An Air Fryer
- Frozen Broccoli
- Salt and Pepper
- Garlic Powder (Optional)
- Olive Oil Spray (Optional)

Directions:
1. Preheat your air fryer at 360 degrees Fahrenheit for 2 minutes.
2. Place the frozen broccoli in the air fryer, do not allow it to thaw before, do not stack them, if your fry basket is large enough, a single layer is perfect.
3. Cook the frozen broccoli at 180°C or 360°F for 4 minutes. This initial cooking phase is mainly to defrost the broccoli.
4. After 4 minutes, remove the fryer basket and empty the water at the bottom of the fryer.
5. Add salt, black pepper, garlic powder (optional), and a few sprays of olive oil to the broccoli.
6. Replace the fry basket and cook for another 4 minutes at the same temperature.
7. Remove the fry basket again and add a sprinkle of parmesan cheese to top it off. Enjoy!

How To Cook Broccoli In Air Fryer

Ingredients:
- An Air fryer
- Broccoli
- Salt and Pepper
- Olive Oil

Directions:
1. Preheat your air fryer to 190°C/375°F for 2 minutes.
2. Cut your broccoli into small florets.
3. Place the broccoli florets into the air fryer basket and add salt, pepper, olive oil and any other seasoning you would like. Toss around all the ingredients to ensure all the broccoli is covered.
4. Cook at 190°C/375°F for 6 minutes.
5. Remove the fry basket and shake it around to ensure even cooking.
6. Replace the fry basket and cook for another 6 minutes at the same temperature.
7. Remove the fry basket again and drizzle a little olive oil if desired. If not, they should be slightly brown and perfectly cooked.

How To Cook Fried Chicken In An Air Fryer

Ingredients:

- Air fryer
- 4 pieces of chicken (your choice – thighs/wings/legs etc)
- 1/2 cup all-purpose flour
- 1 egg
- Salt and pepper

Directions:

1. Mix the flour, salt and pepper in a shallow dish. The amount of salt and pepper you use is up to you, but you probably want to use at least 1 teaspoon of each.
2. Beat the egg in another shallow dish and put it next to the flour mixture.
3. Dredge the chicken in the flour mixture. Then, dip the chicken into the beaten egg. Next, dredge the chicken in the flour mixture once again. Finally, put the chicken in the air fryer's fry basket.
4. Set the air fryer temperature to 200°C/400°F and let it cook for 12 minutes.
5. After the 12 minutes are up, remove the fry basket and use tongs to turn the chicken over. This will ensure that the chicken cooks and browns evenly. Cook for 12 more minutes.
6. After the 12 minutes are up, check the chicken to see if it's crispy enough for you. If it is, then that's it. Enjoy! If not, cook for another 3-5 minutes.

How To Cook Buffalo Wings In An Air Fryer

Servings: 4   Cooking Time: 25 Mins.

Ingredients:

- Airfryer
- 1 kg chicken wings
- 120 ml (1/2 cup) hot sauce/buffalo wings sauce
- 6 Tablespoons melted butter – optional
- 1-2 Tablespoons brown sugar – optional
- 1 Tablespoon Worcestershire Sauce – optional

Directions:

1. Prep the wings by cutting off the tips and separating the drumettes from the wingettes.
2. If you're keeping things simple and just using the hot sauce, you can skip this step.
3. Mix up your sauce by combining the hot sauce, melted butter, brown sugar, and Worcestershire sauce.
4. The butter will make the wings nice and decadent while the brown sugar and Worcestershire sauce will add some depth to the flavour.
5. You can play around with how much of these extra ingredients you add to the hot sauce. Taste test until you get the right flavour. You can also try adding some spices like cayenne pepper and garlic powder for that extra kick.
6. Pour half of the sauce over the wings and stir to make sure the wings are well-covered. For especially flavorful and tender wings, let this marinate in the refrigerator at least a few hours or even overnight – this will allow more of the sauce to be absorbed.
7. Put the wings into the air fryer basket, set the temperature to 190°C/380°F and cook the wings for 20 minutes.
8. After 20 minutes, remove the fry basket and give it a good shake to ensure even cooking, you can also use tongs to turn the wings instead of shaking.
9. Turn the temperature up to 200°C/400°F and cook the wings for another 5 minutes.
10. Remove the wings and coat them with the remaining hot sauce then serve.

How To Cook Chips In An Air Fryer

Servings: 2   **Cooking Time:** 20 to 25 Mins.

Ingredients:
- Air fryer
- 2 large potatoes
- 2-4 Tablespoons olive oil
- Salt

Directions:
1. Scrub the potatoes. Peel, if desired. Cut into strips. Try to make them equally thick. Around 1 centimetre thick is a good size – this ensures that they cook evenly without some being perfect and some being undercooked.
2. Put the cut potatoes in a bowl with some cold water and leave it for about 30 minutes. This helps to remove some of the starch from the potatoes, resulting in chips that cook better and get perfectly brown and crispy.
3. Drain the cut potatoes and pat dry. Drizzle with oil. You can use up to 4 Tablespoons, but 2 Tablespoons will probably be plenty. Toss to combine and make sure the chips are well-coated.
4. Put the chips into the fry basket. Set the temperature to 180°C (350°F). Set the timer for 5 minutes and let it cook.
5. After 5 minutes, remove the fry basket and shake it well. Shaking during cooking makes sure the chips cook and brown evenly – if you have an air fryer that automatically rotates then you can skip this step.
6. Set the timer for another 8 minutes and let the chips cook again.
7. After the 8 minutes are up, stop and shake again.
8. Set the time for another 7 minutes and let it cook again.
9. Check on the chips. If you like them just golden brown and not too crisp, they may be done at this point. If you like them a bit more crispy, shake again and cook for another 5 minutes.
10. Sprinkle with salt and enjoy.

Notes:
1. This air fryer chips recipe is classic and doesn't use unique flavours, but you can easily make these chips more gourmet by adding some spices. Try fresh minced garlic and some parmesan cheese. Or, drizzle the finished chips with some truffle oil.
2. Other spices and herbs can also be used, like basil, thyme, or red pepper. Don't be afraid to get creative. You can substitute a different kind of oil if you wish, avocado oil works quite well.
3. If you want to minimize calories, you can just use a few sprays of cooking spray rather than oil. This air fryer chips recipe uses oil to really mimic the taste of deep-frying, but you can make tasty chips with much less oil. In fact, you can even make these chips with no oil at all. They will, however, end up crispier and a bit drier.

How To Cook Chicken Breast In An Air Fryer

Servings: 2   Cooking Time: 15 Mins.

Ingredients:

- Air fryer
- Meat pounder
- Wax paper or plastic wrap
- 2 skinless/boneless chicken breast halves
- 1 teaspoon salt
- 2 teaspoons paprika
- 2 teaspoons onion powder
- 2 teaspoons black pepper
- 1 teaspoon white pepper
- 1 teaspoon cayenne pepper
- 1 teaspoon ground cumin
- 1 teaspoon ground oregano

Directions:

1. Put your chicken breasts between a few sheets of wax paper or plastic wrap and use a meat pounder until the chicken gets an even thickness. This ensures that the chicken will cook evenly and to your desired level of tenderness.
2. Make the blackened seasoning by mixing the salt, paprika, onion powder, black pepper, white pepper, cayenne pepper, ground cumin, and ground oregano. Make sure the spices are evenly mixed.
3. Dredge the chicken in your blackened seasoning spice mixture.
4. Place the chicken breasts in your fry basket. Turn the temperature to 290°F/150°C and cook for 8 minutes.
5. After 8 minutes, remove the fry basket and turn the chicken breasts over. Set the temperature to 380°F/190°C and cook for 6 more minutes.

Notes:

1. If you don't have a meat pounder, you can use a rolling pin or a large spoon or the bottom of a pot.
2. Alternatively, you can just slice the chicken breast to an even thickness. This may even result in more tender meat than the pounding method. Even thickness, however you get it, is important for cooking perfect chicken.
3. To make this air fryer chicken breast recipe even better, marinate the chicken. You should let it marinate for at least 20 minutes or, ideally, overnight. This will result in juicier, more tender chicken with more flavour. Marinating makes meat perfectly tender and flavorful.
4. You can buy a marinade or make one yourself. A simple marinade might include olive oil, lemon juice, soy sauce, garlic, and some spices. You can buy a Cajun-flavored marinade sauce or you could even use something like Italian salad dressing as a marinade.
5. Another way to simplify this air fryer chicken breast recipe is to use a prepared spice mixture. It's easy to find Cajun blackened spice mixes. This way, you don't have to worry about measuring out the different ingredients but you get the same great taste.

How To Cook Potato Wedges In An Air Fryer

Servings: 4   Cooking Time: 25 Mins.

Ingredients:
- Air fryer
- 4 large potatoes
- 3 Tbsp olive oil
- 3 cloves garlic or 3/4 teaspoon garlic powder
- 1 teaspoon rosemary
- 1/2 teaspoon oregano
- 1/2 teaspoon thyme
- Salt and pepper

Directions:
1. Scrub your potatoes and cut them into wedges. Try to get the thickness of the wedges as consistent as possible, this ensures even cooking and no undercooked or overcooked wedges.
2. Mince or crush your garlic, if using fresh. Combine the olive oil with the garlic and spices. Add salt and pepper. Stir well.
3. Pour the oil and herb mix over the potatoes in a large bowl. Toss to combine, making sure each wedge is well-covered in the oil mix. Put the wedges into the fry basket.
4. Set the air fryer temperature to 190°C/375°F and cook for 8 minutes.
5. After 8 minutes, remove the fry basket and shake it well, this ensures the wedges cook and brown evenly. Set the timer to another 8 minutes and resume cooking.
6. After 8 minutes, stop and shake the fry basket again. Set the timer for another 5 minutes and resume cooking.
7. Check on the wedges. If they are looking brown and crispy, it's time to enjoy them. If not, give them one last shake and set the timer for 3-5 more minutes.

Notes:
1. This air fryer potato wedges recipe calls for dried herbs, but it's even better with fresh herbs. When using fresh herbs, you generally need to triple the quantity.
2. So, for example, you would want to use 1 Tablespoon of fresh minced rosemary instead of 1 teaspoon of dried rosemary.
3. Top the finished wedges with some minced fresh rosemary and thyme or your favourite herbs for a picture-perfect finish and a restaurant-worthy taste.
4. To make these wedges even better, soak the cut potatoes in cold water overnight or for at least 30 minutes. This helps remove some of the starch, resulting in crispier wedges that don't stick together when cooking, it's not an absolutely necessary step but it can definitely elevate the finished product.
5. Another way to potentially elevate this air fryer potato wedges recipe is to reserve some of the oil and herb mix and drizzle it over the finished wedges.
6. It doesn't take much, but a little oil drizzled over the hot and crispy wedges can add a lot of flavour.
7. To make these wedges even lower in calories, you can skip the oil. Instead, just spray the cut potato wedges with some cooking spray and toss them in the herbs before cooking.

How To Cook Burgers In An Air Fryer

Servings: 4   Cooking Time: 8 to 15 Mins.

Ingredients:
- Air fryer
- 300g ground beef
- 1 small onion
- 2 Tablespoons Worcestershire sauce
- 1-2 cloves garlic
- 1/4 cup breadcrumbs
- 1/8 teaspoon cayenne pepper
- 1 egg
- Salt and pepper

Directions:
1. Dice the onion into small pieces.
2. In a large bowl, mix all ingredients together. It works best using your hands. Make sure the meat and seasoning are well combined.
3. Form the burger mixture into 4 patties. Use your thumb to make a good-sized indentation in the center of each patty. This helps the burgers stay uniformly thick and flat during cooking.
4. Place the patties in the fry basket, do not stack them. Set the temperature to 190°C /375° F. Cook for 8 minutes.
5. Check to see how well done the burgers are. Flip them over and cook for another 2-7 minutes, as needed. If you like your burgers more well done, they'll need more time. 10 minutes may be all you need if you like your burgers rare to medium.

Notes:
1. Try adding a few drops of liquid smoke to your burger mix to create a taste similar to a grilled burger from a backyard barbecue.
2. It's important to make sure your ground beef and seasonings are mixed well but don't work the meat too much or the burgers will be tough.
3. To make your burger experience even better, use the air fryer to toast your buns as well. You can also use your air fryer to prepare some tasty burger toppings, like sauteed onions and mushrooms.
4. Optionally, you can spray the tops of your burgers with a little cooking spray before cooking.
5. If you want to make a mouthwatering juicy cheeseburger, just add a slice of cheese on top of each patty for the last few minutes of cooking.
6. Just like when making burgers on the grill, keep checking it to ensure it doesn't burn or get too dry.

How To Cook Onion Rings In An Air Fryer

Servings: 2   Cooking Time: 7 to 10 Mins.

Ingredients:
- Air fryer
- 1 large onion
- 1 cup all-purpose flour
- 1/2 cup bread crumbs
- 1 teaspoon salt
- 1 egg
- 3/4 cup milk

Directions:
1. Cut the onion into 1/4 inch slices and separate them into rings.
2. Mix the flour and salt in a bowl. Dip each onion slice into the flour until well-coated.
3. Add the egg and milk to the flour and whisk until it's well-combined into a batter. If the consistency isn't quite right, add a little extra milk or flour.
4. Spread the bread crumbs on a plate.
5. Dip each flour-coated onion ring into the batter, then dip into the breadcrumbs. Make sure each ring is well-coated with bread crumbs.
6. Put the rings in the air fryer basket. Set the temperature to 190°C/380°F. Cook for 5 minutes.
7. Check the rings and use tongs to turn them over to ensure even browning. Cook for another 3-5 minutes, until the rings are golden brown or to your desired level of crispiness.

Notes:
1. The best onions to use for onion rings are either sweet onions or yellow onions. White onions are a little bit too strong for most people when it comes to onion rings.
2. Try adding a few tablespoons of grated parmesan cheese to the breadcrumbs for a more flavorful breading. You can also add a little pepper and other spices if desired. Garlic powder and parmesan go well together.
3. You can spray the onion rings with a little bit of cooking spray before putting them in the air fryer to achieve a taste that is closer to the deep-fried original.
4. If you're looking for a lower-calorie version, you can skip the flour batter. Just dip each onion ring into an egg white and then into the breadcrumbs. This will result in onion rings that are even healthier, though the taste might be a bit different.
5. This air fryer onion rings recipe works best when making a smaller serving size. To make onion rings for a larger group, you'll need to make them in shifts. The cook time is pretty short, though, so this shouldn't slow you down too much.
6. The exact cooking time will vary depending on how thick your slices are and how well done you like your onion rings.
7. If you prefer them pretty well-browned and crispy, expect it to take a full 10 minutes. If you don't want them to be extremely crispy, they may need only 7 minutes or so.
8. Just be sure to check on the rings after five minutes.

How To Cook Hash Browns In An Air Fryer

🥣 Servings: 2   🍲 Cooking Time: 20 Mins.

Ingredients:
- Air fryer
- 2 Potatoes
- 1 Tablespoon olive oil
- Salt

Directions:
1. Peel the potatoes and either dice or grate them.
2. Put potatoes in a bowl and cover with cold water. Let sit for at least 30 minutes. This will remove some of the starch which will result in potatoes that don't stick together when cooking. It also leads to crispier hash browns.
3. Drain the potatoes and dry them with paper towels or a dishtowel. It's important to get them fairly dry.
4. Drizzle the olive oil over the potatoes and toss to combine. Sprinkle with salt, to taste.
5. Put the potatoes into the fry basket. Set the temperature to 180°C/360°F and cook for 10 minutes.
6. Shake the basket or use tongs to toss the potatoes. This ensures even browning. Cook for 10 more minutes. You might need less time, depending on how browned and crispy you want your hash browns to be.
7. Sprinkle with more salt, to taste, along with any other desired seasonings.

Notes:
1. Try using a mix of salt and garlic salt when seasoning your hash browns. Potatoes and garlic always go well together so this addition will make your hash browns even tastier.
2. You can try using avocado oil instead of olive oil for a slightly different taste.
3. Although both olive oil and avocado oil are healthy oils, avocado is the new winner with its outstanding nutritional profile. It has a pretty neutral taste, so if olive oil isn't your favourite, this is a good alternative.
4. You could also use another oil or fat, like coconut oil or melted butter, just don't add too much.

How To Cook Chicken Nuggets In An Air Fryer

 Servings: 4   Cooking Time: 15 Mins.

Ingredients:
- Air fryer
- Resealable plastic bag
- 250g chicken breast
- 1/2 cup bread crumbs
- 1/2 cup all-purpose flour
- 2 eggs
- 2 Tablespoons olive oil
- Salt & Pepper

Directions:
1. Cut the chicken breast into nugget-sized pieces. Add the chicken pieces to a resealable plastic bag along with the flour. Seal the bag and give it a good shake to make sure the chicken nuggets are evenly coated.
2. Prepare your batter station. Beat the eggs. Next to the eggs, place a bowl with the breadcrumbs. Season the breadcrumbs with some salt and pepper and then mix the olive oil with the breadcrumbs.
3. One at a time, dip each floured piece of chicken into the egg and then into the breadcrumb mixture until it is well-coated.
4. Put the nuggets into your air fryer basket. Set the temperature to 170°C/330°F and cook for 10 minutes.
5. After 10 minutes, remove the fry basket and shake well or use tongs to turn the nuggets over.
6. Set the temperature to 180°C/390°F and cook for another 5 minutes or until the nuggets are golden brown.

Notes:
1. Optionally, you could skip the plastic bag and just flour each piece of chicken by hand.
2. You might want to try seasoning the flour as well, with salt and pepper or even a teaspoon or so of garlic powder.
3. If your nuggets are looking pretty dry at the 10-minute mark, add a little bit of olive oil for the last bit of cooking.
4. After trying this air fryer chicken nuggets recipe once, don't be afraid to try to make it your own.
5. Try adding some different spices to the batter mix, or try different kinds of breadcrumbs until you find which ones you like best.
6. To really try to capture the texture of fast-food chicken nuggets, you might want to use a food processor to puree the chicken.
7. When you do this, you can and should add some spices and an egg to hold everything together.
8. You'll have to form the chicken mixture into nugget shapes before battering, you can even have a little fun with this and make hearts or animal shapes.

How To Cook Salmon In An Air Fryer

Servings: 4   Cooking Time: 20 to 25 Mins.

Ingredients:
- Air fryer
- 4 salmon fillets (about 6 oz. each)
- 3 lemons
- 8 sprigs rosemary
- 1 Tablespoon olive oil
- Salt

Directions:
1. Slice the lemons into thin slices.
2. Arrange several lemon slices on the bottom of the fry basket. Lay 4 rosemary sprigs on top of the lemons.
3. Place one salmon fillet on top of each sprig of rosemary. Sprinkle some salt on the salmon.
4. Top each salmon fillet with another sprig of rosemary. Cover with more lemon slices.
5. Drizzle olive oil over the top of everything.
6. Put the fry basket in the fryer. Set the temperature to 270°F. Set the timer for 20 minutes.
7. Check on the salmon. If it flakes easily with a fork, it's ready to enjoy. If not, put it in for another 5 minutes.
8. Serve the salmon with the roasted lemon slices and rosemary.

Notes:
1. You can probably get away with using less than 1 Tablespoon of olive oil. You should use at least 1 teaspoon, but you don't absolutely need to use the full amount.
2. Cutting out a bit of olive oil is a good way to lower the total calorie count of the dish.
3. You might enjoy this air fried salmon recipe with the addition of garlic. Just mince some fresh garlic and put it on top of the salmon along with rosemary, about one small clove per fillet.
4. Fresh garlic is best but a sprinkle of garlic powder or garlic pepper could also work.
5. Don't have any rosemary? This recipe will also work with just lemons and olive oil. The rosemary adds a nice punch of flavour, but the classic lemon salmon will work well on its own as well. Or, you could try it with other herbs.
6. Parsley, dill, thyme, and basil can all complement salmon quite well. Fresh herbs are best but dried herbs can work also.
7. To create the most flavorful salmon, you could make a pouch to cook the salmon in using tin foil or parchment paper. This seals in all the flavours and results in juicier, more flavorful fish.
8. Both parchment paper and tin foil are safe to use in an air fryer, but it's important to make sure the entire bottom of the fry basket isn't covered. These materials can block the flow of air which is vital for the dish to cook properly.
9. The pouch method in the air fryer might work best when cooking for one rather than making several servings.

How To Make Chocolate Brownies In An Air Fryer

Servings: 16   **Cooking Time: 20 to 25 Mins.**

Ingredients:

- Air fryer
- An Air fryer baking tin
- 1 pack brownie mix
- 3 Tablespoons vegetable oil
- 75ml water
- 1 medium egg

Directions:

1. Pour the brownie mix into a bowl then add the water, vegetable oil and egg. Mix it thoroughly and ensure the mixture doesn't have any lumps.
2. Grease the air fryer baking tin and spread the mixture around to get a consistent level throughout.
3. Set the air fryer to 160°C and let the brownies cook for 20 minutes.
4. After the 20 minutes are up, remove the fry basket and stick a knife into the brownies, if it comes out almost clean the brownies should be finished at this point. If not, cook for another 3 minutes.
5. After 3 minutes, check again, if the knife comes out clean then the brownies are done. Allow to cool off then slice up into squares and enjoy your air fried brownies.

Notes:

1. 3 tablespoons of oil might sound like a lot, but if you're trying to cut out as many calories as possible, 1½ will work perfectly fine – you won't even notice the difference.

How To Cook Frozen Samosa In An Air Fryer

Servings: 2   Cooking Time: 20 Mins.

Ingredients:
- Air fryer
- 4 frozen samosas
- Olive oil spray

Directions:
1. Spray both sides of the samosas with olive oil and place them in the air fryer. Do not stack them, if you have a lot of samosas to cook, do them in batches instead of stacking.
2. Set the timer to 10 minutes and the temperature to 190°C and let it cook.
3. After 10 minutes, remove the fryer basket and shake it around to ensure all the samosas cook evenly.
4. Set the timer to another 10 minutes and let it cook again.
5. Remove the fry basket again and check to see if it's brown and crispy enough for your liking. If not, cook for an additional 2-3 minutes.

How To Cook Meatballs In An Air Fryer

Servings: 6 **Cooking Time: 15 Mins.**

Ingredients:
- Air fryer
- 1 lb lean ground beef
- 1/2 cup bread crumbs
- 1 small onion
- 1 egg
- 1/2 cup Ketchup
- 1/2 teaspoon Worcestershire sauce
- 1 Tablespoon hot sauce
- 1/2 teaspoon salt
- 1/4 teaspoon pepper

Directions:
1. Chop the onion into small pieces.
2. In a large bowl, mix all the ingredients. Using your hands will lead to a blend that is as even as possible. Every meatball should have the same balanced blend of flavours so take the time to mix well. Just be careful not to overwork the meat which can lead to toughness.
3. Using your hands, shape the mixture into 24 balls of equal size. The balls should be about the size of a golf ball. Getting them as even as possible is key so that they all cook evenly.
4. Place half of the meatballs in the air fryer's fry basket. Set the temperature to 190°C/375°F and cook for 15 minutes.
5. Remove the fry basket after 10 minutes and give it a good shake around then replace the fry basket and continue cooking for the last 5 minutes.
6. Repeat the same process for the remaining batch.

Notes:
1. To form perfectly equal meatballs, you can use a cookie scoop or a melon baller. Alternatively, you can form the meatball mixture into a square pan and then cut it into even squares.
2. Each square can then easily be formed into a ball shape. Or, you can be unique and make "meat squares" instead of meatballs!
3. If your air fryer has an issue with food sticking to the bottom of the fry basket, you should spray the bottom of the fry basket with a little cooking spray before making these meatballs.
4. This will also lead to a delicious slightly crisp and caramelized bottom to each meatball, so it might be worth doing even if your fryer doesn't have an issue with food sticking.
5. Feel free to experiment and get creative with your ingredients. This air fryer meatballs recipe uses classic meatball flavours, but there are endless ways you could make these meatballs unique.
6. Try adding some minced garlic or add a little sweetness with some brown sugar or throw in some Asian flavours.
7. This air fryer meatballs recipe works great for party snacks. For ease of serving, just insert a toothpick into each meatball.
8. You can try a mixture of different meats, like beef, veal, and pork, and you can also try turkey or chicken meatballs for a healthier option.

How To Cook Chicken Wings In An Air Fryer

Servings: 2   Cooking Time: 25 to 30 Mins.

Ingredients:
- Air fryer
- 2 lbs. chicken wings
- 5 Tablespoons olive oil
- 1/4 cup sriracha sauce
- 1 lime
- 1/4 cup honey
- 2 cloves garlic
- 1 teaspoon ground cumin

Directions:
1. Mince or crush the garlic cloves.
2. Juice and zest the lime.
3. Prepare your spicy sauce by combining the garlic, lime juice, lime zest, ground cumin, olive oil, sriracha sauce, and honey. Whisk with a fork to make sure it's well mixed.
4. Prepare your chicken wings by cutting off the tips and separating the drummettes and flats.
5. Keep a small amount of the sauce, pour the remaining sauce mixture over the wings and toss until they are well-coated.
6. Set the air fryer's temperature to 180°C/360°F. Set the timer to 10 minutes and let it cook.
7. After 10 minutes, flip the wings over. Set the timer for another 10 minutes and resume cooking.
8. When the 10 minutes are up, flip the wings again. Brush the tops of the wings with some of the reserved sauce mix. Set the timer for 5 more minutes and let it cook again.
9. Check the wings. If they are browned and crisp, they're ready to enjoy. If not they may need up to 5 more minutes.

Notes:
1. Optionally, finish your wings off with some fresh minced cilantro for a nice touch. If you're a big cilantro lover, you can also add some minced cilantro to the sriracha sauce mix before cooking.
2. You can also serve the wings with lime wedges, as a fresh squeeze of lime on top complements the heat of the wings quite well.
3. If you're all about the spicy and don't need any sweetness to balance it, feel free to skip the honey. The honey helps lower the overall heat of these wings and provides a nice balance of flavours.
4. These wings are still plenty spicy with the honey, but without the honey, you'll really taste the fire.
5. If this isn't spicy enough for you, add in 1-2 teaspoons of cayenne pepper. If that's still not spicy enough for you, puree your spice mix with one whole serrano chilli pepper and a few whole jalapeno peppers.
6. Take this air fryer chicken wings recipe to the next level by marinating your wings overnight in the sriracha sauce mix for wings that are even more flavorful and extra tender.

Chicken And Bacon Burger

Servings: 4 **Cooking Time:** 10 to 30 Mins.

Ingredients:

- 4 skinless, boneless chicken breasts
- 2 garlic cloves, grated
- 2 tbsp olive oil
- 8 rashers smoked streaky bacon
- 4 large wholemeal burger buns
- 2 Little Gem lettuces, leaves separated
- 2 large tomatoes, sliced
- 1 ripe avocado, quartered and sliced
- salt and freshly ground black pepper
- For the ranch dressing
- 2 tbsp reduced-fat mayonnaise
- 2 tbsp soured cream
- ½ garlic clove, finely grated
- 2 tbsp finely chopped dill
- 1 tbsp finely chopped chives
- 3 dashes Worcestershire sauce
- pinch cayenne pepper
- 2 dashes Sriracha hot sauce
- ½ tsp white wine vinegar
- 1 tsp mild American mustard

Directions:

1. Preheat the oven to 200C/180C Fan/Gas 6 and line a baking tray with baking paper.
2. Put the chicken breasts on a board lined with clingfilm. Top with another layer of clingfilm and bash with a rolling pin to a 1cm/½in even thickness. Lay the chicken breasts in a shallow dish. Add the garlic, olive oil and some salt and pepper and rub well into the chicken. Set aside to marinate for 15 minutes.
3. Meanwhile, lay the bacon rashers on a wire rack over the lined baking tray. Cook in the oven for 12–15 minutes, or until browned and crispy.
4. For the ranch dressing, mix all the ingredients together and season with salt and pepper.
5. Heat a large griddle pan over a high heat. Cut the burger buns in half and toast the cut sides on the griddle in batches, until lightly charred. Set aside.
6. Lay the chicken breasts on the griddle and cook for 2–3 minutes on each side, or until cooked through.
7. To assemble the burgers, spread 1 tablespoon of ranch dressing over the bottom of each burger bun. Add the lettuce, chicken, tomato, bacon and avocado. Spread some more ranch dressing on the top half of the burger bun. Place on top of the filling and serve.

Fried Chicken Sandwich

Servings: 1   **Cooking Time:** 10 to 30 Mins.

Ingredients:

- For the pink-pickled onions
- ½ red onion, thinly sliced
- red wine vinegar or lime juice to cover
- For the fried chicken
- 75ml/2½fl oz kefir, buttermilk or plain yoghurt
- ½ tsp hot smoked paprika, plus ¼ tsp for the coating
- ½ tsp fine sea salt, plus ¼ tsp for the coating
- 1 tsp lemon juice
- ½ tsp Dijon mustard
- ½ tsp maple syrup
- 1 fat garlic clove, finely grated
- 1 small boneless chicken thigh fillet, skin removed
- 4–5 tbsp plain flour
- sunflower oil for deep-frying
- To serve
- 4 tbsp garlic mayonnaise
- 1 tsp crispy chilli oil or other chilli sauce
- ¼ tsp honey
- 1 burger bun, split, or 2 slices white bread
- a few leaves iceberg lettuce
- kimchi or pickles of your choice

Directions:

1. Make your pink-pickled onions in advance: at least 2 hours, and up to 24. Put the onion into a jar or bowl and cover with the vinegar (or lime juice), pressing down on the onions. Cover and leave the onions to steep.

2. Pour the kefir, buttermilk or yoghurt into a small dish and stir in the ½ teaspoon of paprika, ½ teaspoon of salt, lemon juice, mustard, maple syrup and garlic. Add the chicken and turn to coat in the marinade. Cover the dish, then leave in the fridge for at least 4 hours or up to 2 days. (If you simply cannot wait that long, leave the chicken out on the kitchen counter for 20–40 minutes.)

3. Take the chicken out of the fridge in good time to get to room temperature before you start to cook it.

4. Mix the flour with the remaining ¼ teaspoon each of paprika and salt in a shallow dish. Lift the chicken out of the marinade, but don't try and shake it off. Dredge both sides of the chicken in the seasoned flour, then dip briefly back into the marinade and dredge again. This double-dredging is essential to get a thick, shaggy coating. You can leave the coated chicken in the flour dish until you fry.

5. Mix the garlic mayonnaise with the chilli oil and honey, and spread over both sides of a split burger bun (or a couple of slices of bread). Put a plate lined with kitchen paper by (but not dangerously near) the hob, if you want to get rid of any excess fat once the chicken's cooked.

6. Pour enough oil into a deep, heavy-bottomed saucepan to come about 3½cm/1 1/3 in up the sides. Heat until a small piece of bread becomes golden and crisp almost instantly; if you have a food thermometer, you want the fat to be at 190°C when the chicken goes in. (CAUTION: hot oil can be dangerous. Do not leave unattended.) Using tongs, gently lower the chicken into the hot oil, and cook for 3–4 minutes on each side, until the coating is deep gold and very crisp and the chicken is completely cooked through. Drain on the paper-lined plate and leave to stand (for a couple of minutes) while you shred some iceberg lettuce and get out your pickles.

7. Put a handful of lettuce on the mayo on the bottom of the bun, top with the fried chicken, add kimchi and pink-pickled onions, scatter with a bit more lettuce and squidge on the top of the bun. Go in cautiously: I have more than once burned my mouth.

Pork Chops With Sloe Sauce And Savoy Cabbage

Servings: 2   **Cooking Time: 30 Mins. to 1 Hour**

Ingredients:

- 1 small Savoy cabbage (about 400g/14oz), core removed, leaves shredded
- 1–2 tbsp virgin rapeseed oil
- 2 pork chops (each about 250g/9oz)
- 1 tsp olive oil
- salt and freshly ground black pepper
- For the sauce
- handful of sloes or bullaces (approximately 100g/3½oz)
- 15g/½oz butter (only needed if the pork chops don't yield much fat)
- 1 banana shallot, finely chopped
- 1 large garlic clove, finely chopped or grated
- 100ml/3½fl oz red wine
- few sprigs fresh thyme
- 100–120ml/3½–4fl oz chicken or other meat stock
- 1 tbsp runny honey or soft brown sugar

Directions:

1. Put the cabbage in a large lidded pan. Cover with water and boil for 3 minutes. Drain and return to the pan. Add the rapeseed oil and stir to coat the cabbage. Season with salt and pepper. Cover and cook over a very low heat, stirring the cabbage every now and again, for 20 minutes or until softened.

2. Rub the chops with the olive oil and season on both sides with salt and pepper. Cook for 4–6 minutes on each side (depending on thickness), until cooked through, or until they reach an internal temperature of 71C. Make sure you brown the fat along the edge. Cover with kitchen foil and rest for about 5 minutes while you make the sauce. Reserve a tablespoon of pork fat from the pan.

3. To make the sauce, stone the sloes using your fingers or a cherry stoner (alternatively, stone them after cooking, which is messy but easier). Put in a small pan and add just enough water to cover (approximately 150ml/¼ pint). Bring to the boil, then reduce the heat and poach for a few minutes to allow them to break down a little. Set aside.

4. In another saucepan, heat the reserved pork fat (if the chops haven't yielded much fat, add the butter). Add the shallot and garlic and cook for 1–2 minutes. Stir in the remaining ingredients and the poached fruit, including any poaching water. Bring to the boil, then simmer for 3–5 minutes. Taste the sauce and add a little more honey or sugar, if needed. Season to taste with salt and pepper.

5. Serve the sauce over the rested pork chops, alongside the cabbage.

Notes:

1. Sloes are very seasonal and ready to be picked in October and November. Traditionally they were picked after the first frost, but you could pick them earlier and freeze to mimic that first frost. The theory behind this is that the frost splits the skins so the juices are released easily when cooking.

2. You can use frozen sloes in this recipe, they will just take a little longer to cook down. You'll need to remove the stones after cooking.

Fish And Chips With Tartare Sauce

Servings: 4   Cooking Time: 10 to 30 Mins.

Ingredients:

- 2 egg yolks
- 1 tbsp Dijon mustard
- 3 tbsp white wine vinegar
- 200ml/7fl oz vegetable oil, plus extra for deep-frying
- squeeze lemon juice
- ½ red onion, chopped
- 1 tbsp gherkins, roughly chopped
- 1 tbsp capers, roughly chopped
- small handful parsley, finely chopped
- 4–5 green olives, chopped
- 12 tbsp plain flour
- 6 tbsp cornflour
- 200ml/7fl oz ale
- pinch salt
- 8 large Maris Piper potatoes, peeled and cut into chunky chips
- 4 x 150g/5½oz cod (or haddock) fillets

Directions:

1. First make the tartare sauce. Whisk together the egg yolks, mustard and vinegar and gradually pour in the oil in a steady stream until you have a thick, creamy mayonnaise. Season to taste and add a squeeze of lemon.
2. Stir in the onion, gherkins, capers, parsley and olives. The sauce should be quite piquant and chunky and have the consistency of very thick double cream.
3. To make the batter, mix the flours together and whisk in the ale until you have a double cream consistency. Add a pinch of salt.
4. Heat the oil in a deep-fat fryer to 140C (CAUTION: hot oil can be dangerous. Do not leave unattended.). Cook the chips for 8–9 minutes and set aside on kitchen paper.
5. Increase the heat to 190C. In batches, dip the fish fillets in the batter and drop carefully into the hot oil. Shake the basket gently so the fillets don't stick, and cook for about 3–5 minutes. Don't overload the basket or the oil will cool and you'll get soggy batter. Remove and drain on kitchen paper.
6. Return the chips to the deep-fat fryer a further 2–3 minutes and drain on kitchen paper. Serve with the battered fish and the tartare sauce.

How To Make Fish Pie

🍲 Servings: 4   🍲 Cooking Time: 30 Mins. to 1 Hour

Ingredients:
- For the mashed potatoes
- 1kg/2lb 4oz potatoes, cut into 5cm/2in chunks
- 50g/2oz butter
- 100g/3½ oz crème fraîche
- 3 tbsp warm milk
- pinch salt and white pepper
- For the filling
- 500ml/1 pint milk
- 250g/9oz smoked haddock
- 200g/7oz cod loin
- 1 onion
- 1 bay leaf
- 3 cloves (optional)
- 2 leeks, washed and chopped
- 50g/2oz butter, plus 25g/1oz for dotting on top of the pie
- 1 tbsp olive oil
- 3 tbsp plain flour
- 100g/3½oz raw king prawns
- 50g/2oz frozen peas
- 1 tbsp finely chopped parsley
- 1 unwaxed lemon, finely grated zest only

Directions:
1. Preheat the oven to 190C/170C Fan/Gas 5.
2. Boil potatoes until tender. Drain and mash them with the butter, crème fraîche and warm milk and season with salt and pepper. Set aside and keep warm.
3. Heat the milk in a large pan, then add the smoked haddock and cod. Cut the onion in half, make an incision in one of the halves and insert the bay leaf. Push the cloves into the same onion half and place this into the pan with the milk and fish. Bring the milk to the boil, then reduce the heat and simmer gently for 6–7 minutes.
4. Meanwhile, finely chop the remaining onion half and the leeks. Heat the butter with the olive oil in a small frying pan and gently fry the onion and leeks for 4–5 minutes, until softened but not browned.
5. Remove the fish from the pan, and set aside to cool slightly. Keep the milk in the pan.
6. Add the flour to the leeks and stir well. Fry for 1 minute, stirring frequently. Gradually spoon in the milk from poaching the fish, and stir it in well each time. Add all the milk in this way, and heat gently until the sauce has thickened. Taste the sauce for seasoning, and add more salt or pepper if necessary.
7. Break the fish into chunks, being careful to feel for any bones and remove any skin, then fold the fish pieces into the sauce. Add the raw prawns and frozen peas to the mixture.
8. Place an ovenproof pie dish onto a baking tray (this will catch any of the mix that bubbles over when cooking). Spoon the fish mixture into the bottom of the dish. Sprinkle the parsley and lemon zest over the top.
9. Carefully top with the cooled mashed potato. Use a fork to spread the mash over the pie and create a rough texture on top. Dot the pie with the remaining half of the butter and place in the oven for 25–30 minutes, or until golden-brown and bubbling.

Notes:
1. You can make the mash for this fish pie recipe in advance. (Mash freezes really well.) Frozen fish works brilliantly and can be poached directly from frozen. A frozen fish pie mix comes in very handy.

Roast Pork And Veg With Gravy

🥣 Servings: 4-6   🍲 Cooking Time: 30 Mins. to 1 Hour

Ingredients:

- 1.2kg–1.5kg/2lb 11oz–3lb 5oz pork shoulder joint, rind scored
- 4 tbsp vegetable oil
- 800g/1lb 12oz potatoes, peeled and cut into 4cm/1½in chunks
- 6 medium carrots, peeled and halved lengthways
- 4 medium parsnips, peeled and halved lengthways
- ½ green cabbage, such as Savoy, trimmed and shredded
- 200g/7oz frozen peas
- salt and ground black pepper
- For the gravy
- 3 tbsp plain flour
- 450ml/16fl oz hot beef or pork stock, made with 1 stock cube

Directions:

1. Preheat the oven to 200C/180C Fan/Gas 6. Place the pork on a board, fat-side down and snip off the trussing string. Your meat should unroll into a large rectangle piece. If it doesn't, cut horizontally through the thickest part with a knife and open the pork up like a book. Season on all sides with salt and pepper.
2. Put the potatoes in a large bowl and toss with 2 tbsp of the oil, a little salt and lots of freshly ground black pepper. Scatter over a large roasting tin. Place the pork in the same roasting tin, fat-side up, nestling in between the potatoes in its flatter, longer shape (not all the pork will have fat or rind once opened out, but this is fine). Roast for 20 minutes.
3. Put the carrots and parsnips in the same bowl that was used to toss the potatoes, drizzle with the remaining oil, season with salt and pepper and toss well together. Scatter over another baking tray.
4. After 20 minutes, turn the potatoes. Return the tray to the oven and add the tray with the carrots and parsnips a couple of rungs below it to allow the hot air to circulate.
5. Cook for a further 30–40 minutes or until the pork is cooked and the vegetables are tender and lightly browned. The pork is cooked when it is hot throughout and the juices run clear when it is pierced with a skewer through the thickest part. The time taken to cook the pork will depend on weight and shape.
6. Transfer the pork to a large board or platter. Cover with kitchen foil and leave to rest for at least 15 minutes. Add the potatoes to the tray with the vegetables, reserving the pork juices, turn off the oven and keep warm.
7. Spoon off all but one tablespoon of the juices from the pork roasting tin and stir in the flour, followed by around a third of the stock. Mix well, lifting as much of the tasty sediment as possible from the base of the tin as it will add lots of flavour to your gravy.
8. Transfer to a saucepan, add the remaining stock then bring to a gentle simmer and cook for 2–3 minutes, stirring. Adjust the seasoning with salt and pepper, then strain through a sieve into a warmed gravy jug.
9. While the gravy is simmering, put the cabbage and peas into a large wide-based microwave-proof dish, cover and cook on high for 5–7 minutes, or until the vegetables are tender, stirring after 3 minutes. (You can also boil the cabbage and peas together in a large saucepan until tender, then drain.)
10. Carve the pork thinly and serve with the vegetables and gravy.

Banana Chips

These crispy, chewy banana chips are great as a snack, or sprinkle them over your morning porridge instead of fresh banana. Our method is oven baked – see our recipe tip below for an air fryer version.

Servings: 3-4   **Cooking Time: 1 to 2 Hours**

Ingredients:

- 2–3 large, almost ripe bananas, peeled and thinly sliced (3mm/no more than ⅛in thick) on a sharp diagonal
- light rapeseed, vegetable or sunflower oil
- 1 lemon, juice only
- ground cinnamon (optional)

Directions:

1. Preheat the oven to 120C/100C Fan/Gas ½. Line a large baking sheet with baking paper and brush all over very lightly with oil.
2. Put the banana slices into a bowl, drizzle over the lemon juice and gently stir to coat.
3. Lift the banana slices from the juice and place on the baking sheet in a single layer. Sprinkle over a few pinches of cinnamon if you like, then bake for 1 hour.
4. Carefully peel the slices from the paper, turn over and bake for a further 30–40 minutes. The slices should feel dry on both sides – they'll crisp up some more as they cool.
5. Leave to cool completely before serving or storing in an airtight container.

Notes:

1. As a snack for adults, sprinkle with a little salt.
2. To air-fry, coat the banana slices in lemon juice as above. Lightly oil or oil-spray the air fryer basket. Add some banana slices in a single layer, then air-fry at 100C for 20 minutes. Carefully turn and rotate the slices and continue to cook for 5 minutes at a time, removing them as they feel crisp and dried out (remove any that have browned too much even if they don't feel crisp – they will crisp more as they cool). Repeat until all the banana slices are crisp – this should take no more than 30 minutes.

Air Fryer Roast Chicken

You can make a delicious and succulent roast chicken in an air fryer, in little over an hour. Here, the bird sits upside down for half of the cooking time so the breast is kept moist. The skin crisps up perfectly for a lovely golden finish, too.

Servings: 4   Cooking Time: 1 to 2 Hours

Ingredients:
- 20g/¾oz butter, softened
- 1 good quality whole chicken, weighing 1.4–1.5kg/3lb 2oz–3lb 5oz
- ½ lemon
- 2 garlic cloves, left whole
- handful thyme or few rosemary sprigs
- salt and freshly ground black pepper

Directions:
1. Heat the air fryer to 180C and rub the butter all over the skin of the chicken. Season well with salt and pepper.
2. Place the lemon half, garlic and thyme in the cavity of the chicken.
3. Roast, breast side down, for 30 minutes. Then flip the right way up and roast for another 35 minutes. Check the chicken is thoroughly cooked and the juices run clear when the thickest parts of the breast and thigh are pierced with a skewer or knife.
4. Leave the chicken to stand for a few minutes before carving. If you would like to make gravy, see the Recipe Tips.

Notes:
1. If you can't fit a whole chicken in your air fryer, use halves or pieces instead. For halves, take a whole chicken and use strong scissors or a boning knife to cut down the spine. Then flip over and cut down the middle of the breast. You'll be left with two halves to fit snugly inside your air fryer. Proceed with step 2, check after 45 minutes and every 5 minutes thereafter until the chicken is cooked through. For pieces, use 2 chicken thighs or drumsticks per person. Mix the butter with a teaspoon of olive oil to loosen and add a squeeze of lemon juice and about 1 teaspoon thyme leaves, then season well. Spread this paste over the chicken pieces and cook in the air fryer at 180C for 10 minutes then turn and cook for another 12–15 minutes until crispy and golden.
2. The juices from the roast chicken in the air fryer can be used to make a gravy. Add a little water to loosen any bits stuck to the base, then pour into a saucepan. Add a little flour and chicken stock or wine and whisk over a medium heat until thickened.
3. Leftover roast chicken will freeze in an airtight container for up to 3 months.
4. This recipe was developed using a 5.5 litre/9½ pint air fryer.

Air Fryer Crispy Chicken Burger

Pimp your BLT with a C for chicken coated in spicy cornflakes and cooked in the air fryer, all sandwiched in a brioche burger bun.

Servings: 2   Cooking Time: 10 to 30 Mins.

Ingredients:
- 2 skinless chicken breasts
- 70g/2½oz cornflakes, crushed
- 1 tsp Cajun seasoning
- 1 tsp paprika
- 1 tsp dried oregano
- 1 tsp lemon salt (optional, see recipe tip)
- 2 free-range eggs
- 2 slices bacon, or more, to taste
- To serve
- 2 brioche burger buns
- light mayonnaise
- iceberg lettuce
- sliced tomato
- 2 tsp pesto (optional)

Directions:
1. Put the chicken breasts on a board and cover with baking paper. Bash them with a rolling pin until they are about 2cm/¾in thick all over.
2. In a shallow bowl, mix the cornflakes with the Cajun seasoning, paprika, oregano and lemon salt, if using.
3. Break the eggs into another shallow bowl and whisk with a fork.
4. Dip the chicken into the eggs until evenly coated, then dip into the cornflakes, ensuring it is fully coated.
5. Air fry at 170C for 17 minutes; check after 15 minutes and lower the temperature if the cornflakes are getting too brown.
6. If your air fryer has one basket, add the bacon 5 minutes after you start cooking the chicken, and cook for 10–12 minutes at 170C. If your air fryer has two baskets, cook the bacon separately at 200C for 8–10 minutes.
7. To assemble, spread some mayo on the bottom halves of the brioche buns. Top with the lettuce, bacon, chicken, sliced tomato and pesto, if using, add the top halves of the buns and serve hot.

Notes:
1. Lemon salt is available in some large supermarkets and from online suppliers. You can make your own by mixing lemon zest with coarse salt in a pestle and mortar.

Air Fryer Chicken Wings With Honey And Sesame

The key to cooking delicious, crispy chicken wings every time in an air fryer is to fry them in a mix of oil, cornflour and seasoning until their skins crisp before tossing them in a sticky glaze and cooking again briefly.

Servings: 1-2   **Cooking Time:** 10 to 30 Mins.

Ingredients:
- 450–500g/1lb–1lb 2oz chicken wings with tips removed
- 1 tbsp olive oil
- 3 tbsp cornflour
- 1 tbsp runny honey
- 1 tsp soy sauce or tamari
- 1 tsp rice wine vinegar
- 1 tsp toasted sesame oil
- 2 tsp sesame seeds, toasted
- 1 large spring onion, thinly sliced
- salt and freshly ground black pepper

Directions:
1. In a large bowl, toss together the chicken wings, olive oil and a generous amount of salt and pepper. Toss in the cornflour, a tablespoon at a time, until the wings are well coated.
2. Air-fry the chicken wings in a single layer for 25 minutes at 180C, turning halfway through the cooking time.
3. Meanwhile, make the glaze by whisking together the honey, soy sauce, rice wine vinegar and toasted sesame oil in a large bowl.
4. Tip the cooked wings into the glaze, tossing until they're well coated. Return to the air fryer in a single layer for 5 more minutes.
5. Toss the wings once more in any remaining glaze. Sprinkle with toasted sesame seeds and spring onion and serve.

Notes:
1. This recipe was tested in a 3.2 litre/5½ pint basket air fryer. It will also work in a model fitted with a stirring paddle, and you won't need to turn the wings halfway. However, some of the coating may fall off the wings as they turn: this will still result in delicious wings, and you'll also get crispy bits, but they may be a little less crisp overall. This recipe is also easily scaled up to feed more people in a larger air fryer.

Air Fryer Fish And Chips With Tartare Sauce

The air fryer gives you crispy fish and chips without the hassle of deep frying, and a touch of rosemary salt takes this favourite supper to a new level.

Servings: 2   Cooking Time: 10 to 30 Mins.

Ingredients:

- 350g/12oz potatoes, such as Maris Piper or King Edward, sliced into 5mm/¼in-thick chips
- 3 tbsp olive oil
- 2 x hake, cod loin or haddock fillets, skinless and boneless (approx. 150g/5½oz each)
- 2 tbsp plain flour
- 1 free-range egg
- 60g/2¼oz panko breadcrumbs (see recipe tip)
- salt and freshly ground black pepper
- lemon wedges to serve (optional)
- For the rosemary salt
- 10g/1/3 oz fresh rosemary, stalks discarded
- 3 tbsp sea salt
- 1 lemon, zest only
- For the tartare sauce
- 3 tbsp mayonnaise
- 1 tbsp Greek-style yoghurt
- ½ lemon, juice only
- 1 tbsp capers
- 5 cocktail gherkins, finely chopped
- 1 tbsp flatleaf parsley, roughly chopped
- pinch smoked paprika

Directions:

1. Preheat the air fryer to 190C.
2. Rinse the chips in cold water for a couple of minutes, then drain and pat dry.
3. Put the chips in a bowl, pour over 2 tablespoons olive oil and mix until all the chips are coated. Air-fry the chips for 15–18 minutes, shaking two to three times during cooking.
4. While the chips are cooking, make the rosemary salt. Blitz the rosemary, salt and lemon zest a small blender, or pound in a pestle and mortar, to form a fragrant green salt; set aside.
5. To make the tartare sauce, mix all the ingredients together in a small bowl.
6. To prepare the fish, put the flour in a bowl and season with salt and pepper. In a second bowl, whisk the egg with some salt and pepper. Put the breadcrumbs in a third bowl.
7. Take one piece of fish and coat both sides in the flour, then dip into the egg and then into the breadcrumbs, turning to coat evenly. Set aside on a plate. Repeat with the second piece of fish.
8. Once the chips are cooked, tip them into a bowl and sprinkle over a couple of pinches of rosemary salt; set aside.
9. Drizzle 1 tablespoon olive oil over the fish and air-fry for 6 minutes. Turn the fish over and cook for another 2–4 minutes, depending on the thickness of the fish.
10. Put the fish onto serving plates. Pop the chips back in the air fryer for 2 minutes to warm up.
11. Serve the fish with the chips and a big dollop of tartare sauce, with lemon wedges if liked.

Notes:

1. Panko breadcrumbs are very light and crisp; alternatively, use leftover bread, blitzed to fine crumbs.
2. Keep any leftover rosemary salt in a small airtight container.

Air Fryer Spicy Pork Belly

Cooking pork belly slices in an air fryer guarantees a crispy outside and succulent meat inside. Once you've made this sticky, sweet and spicy marinade you'll be making it every week!

Servings: 4   **Cooking Time: 10 to 30 Mins.**

Ingredients:
- 3 tbsp light soy sauce
- 1½ tbsp cider or wine vinegar
- 1 tbsp vegetable oil
- 2 garlic cloves, crushed or finely grated
- ½ tsp dried chilli flakes
- 2 tsp Chinese five-spice powder
- 2 tsp runny honey or sugar
- ½ tsp salt
- 500g/1lb 2oz pork belly slices
- freshly cooked rice and steamed greens, to serve

Directions:
1. Mix together the soy sauce, vinegar, oil, garlic, chilli flakes, Chinese five-spice, sugar and salt together in a large shallow dish. Add the pork slices and leave to marinate at room temperature for 10–15 minutes.
2. Preheat the air fryer to 180C. Arrange the pork slices in the air fryer basket, ideally in a single layer. Air-fry for 25–30 minutes, turning halfway through and brushing with any remaining marinade, until the pork is well browned and completely cooked through.
3. Serve the pork with the rice and steamed greens.

Notes:
1. To make a little extra sauce to drizzle over the cooked pork, stir together 1 tablespoon soy sauce, ½ tablespoon vinegar and 1 tablespoon water.
2. If you don't have an air fryer you can cook this in an oven preheated to 200C/180C Fan/Gas 6 for 45–55 minutes, basting and turning every 15 minutes.

Air Fryer Chicken Parmigiana

A firm family favourite, this is traditionally served with spaghetti but it is just as delicious with a simple crisp green salad.

Servings: 2 **Cooking Time: 10 to 30 Mins.**

Ingredients:

- For the tomato sauce
- 1 small garlic clove, sliced
- ½ onion, thinly sliced
- 1 small carrot, peeled, halved lengthwise and thinly sliced
- 100g/3½oz cherry tomatoes, halved
- olive oil spray
- 1 basil sprig (or small handful basil leaves)
- salt and freshly ground black pepper

- For the chicken
- 2 chicken breasts
- 1 large free-range egg, beaten
- 50g/1¾oz panko breadcrumbs
- 15g/½oz Parmesan, finely grated
- 50g/1¾oz mozzarella, sliced
- small handful parsley leaves, roughly chopped, to garnish

Directions:

1. To make the sauce, heat the air fryer to 200C. In a heatproof tray or bowl that will fit inside the air fryer, mix together the garlic, onion, carrot and cherry tomatoes. Spray a few times with the olive oil spray and season well with salt and pepper. Cook for 8–10 minutes, until soft. Transfer to a blender or food processor, add the basil and blend to a smooth purée. Set aside.
2. To make the chicken, lay the chicken breasts on a piece of baking paper and cover with another sheet of baking paper. Use the end of a rolling pin to bash the breasts until about 2cm/¾in thick.
3. Heat the air fryer to 205C. Place the egg in a small, wide bowl. Mix the panko breadcrumbs with most of the Parmesan, reserving about 2 teaspoons, in a wide bowl or large plate.
4. Dip the chicken breasts first into the egg mixture and then into the Parmesan breadcrumbs. Press well to ensure a good, even coating (if there are any uncoated patches, dip into the egg and breadcrumbs again).
5. Lay the chicken breasts in the air fryer (you may need to do one at a time, depending on the size of your air fryer) and cook for 10 minutes, turning the chicken over after 6 minutes.
6. When the chicken is golden and cooked through, remove from the air fryer and spoon half of the tomato sauce over each breast, then top with the mozzarella and a sprinkling of the reserved Parmesan. Return to the air fryer for 3 minutes to melt the cheese, then remove and garnish with the parsley.

Notes:

1. To roast the vegetables for the sauce, use a springform cake tin that fits inside the air fryer or a square baking tin for a square basket. Alternatively, use greaseproof air fryer liners.
2. The tomato sauce can be made ahead of time. The chicken is crispiest and best served immediately.
3. As chicken breasts vary in size, you may need a little more liquid for the coating if you have large pieces. Add a few tablespoons of milk to the beaten eggs if needed.
4. This recipe was developed using a 5.5 litre/9½ pint air fryer.

Air Fryer Falafel

A fantastic way to make falafel with a fraction of the oil, but all the crisp, hot, garlickiness that you want. Load up with sauces, pickles and chilli to your taste.

Servings: 2   **Cooking Time: 10 to 30 Mins.**

Ingredients:

- 400g tin chickpeas, drained
- 1 red onion, roughly chopped
- 3 garlic cloves, chopped
- handful chopped fresh coriander
- 2 tsp ground cumin
- 1 lemon, zest and juice
- 1 tsp salt
- 2 tbsp olive oil
- 50g/1¾oz gram flour
- spray oil, or more olive oil
- To serve
- 4 flatbreads
- chilli sauce, to taste
- handful pickled chillies
- 1 carrot, grated
- pickled red cabbage, to taste
- tahini sauce, roasted red pepper hummus and/or yoghurt, to taste
- few sprigs coriander, mint or parsley, to serve

Directions:

1. In a food processor, blend the drained chickpeas, red onion, garlic, coriander, cumin, lemon juice, lemon zest, salt and olive oil - pulse until the mixture is still rough but holding together. (You can mash the mixture with a sturdy potato masher, but you will need to chop the onions and garlic very finely.)
2. Using your hands, form into balls. Sprinkle the gram flour onto a plate and roll the balls in the flour, lightly coating them.
3. Spray your air fryer with oil before cooking to avoid sticking. (You can also spray the falafels if you like.) Place the falafels into the air fryer and cook at 190C for about 15 minutes – please note that the cooking time may vary depending on the particular brand of air fryer.
4. Serve a couple of falafels inside each flatbread, loaded with all the toppings you like – pickled chillies, grated carrot, pickled red cabbage, tahini sauce and hummus or yoghurt dip.

Air Fryer Chips

While undoubtedly you can make the best restaurant-style French fries by cooking frozen chips in an air fryer, you can also produce delicious chunky, chip-shop-style chips made entirely from scratch. Any potato will work but waxy varieties are best for this recipe, and if you have any leftover potatoes where the skins are starting to go soft these will taste almost exactly like they came from the local chippy.

Servings: 2   Cooking Time: 10 to 30 Mins.

Ingredients:
- 2 large potatoes (approximately 450g/1lb), preferably a waxy variety
- 1 tbsp olive oil
- salt, to taste

Directions:
1. Leaving the skins on, cut the potatoes into roughly 1cm/½in thick chips. Toss with the olive oil and a generous amount of salt.
2. Air-fry for 20–30 minutes at 180C, tossing every 10 minutes or so until the chips are crisp and golden, making sure they don't stick to the bottom of the basket towards the beginning of cooking.

Notes:
1. If you have time, soak the chips for up to 30 minutes to extract some of the starch before frying. You can also par-boil the chips for 8–10 minutes to cut the cooking time and make really fluffy chips. This recipe was tested in a 3.2 litre/5½ pint basket air fryer, but it will also work in a model fitted with a stirring paddle – in this case, you won't need to toss the chips during cooking.

Air Fryer Chicken Fajitas

Spicy, colourful chicken fajita wraps are so quick and easy to make in the air fryer, you can whip them up at any time of day. Make your own guacamole or use shop-bought. You could skip the wraps and have the spicy chicken with crisp tacos or rice instead.

Servings: 2 **Cooking Time: 10 to 30 Mins.**

Ingredients:

- 3 skinless chicken breasts, sliced into strips
- 1 red pepper, seeds removed, sliced
- 1 yellow pepper, seeds removed, sliced
- 1 red chilli, seeds removed, sliced
- 1 tbsp vegetable oil
- 1 tsp garlic granules
- 1 tsp ground cumin
- 1 tbsp paprika
- 1 tsp Cajun seasoning
- 1 tsp ground coriander
- salt
- To serve
- 4 tortilla wraps, warmed
- 200g/7oz guacamole
- 8 tsp soured cream

Directions:

1. Coat the chicken, peppers and chilli in the oil, spices and salt.
2. Air-fry at 200C for 15 minutes, shaking the air fryer basket twice during this time.
3. Divide the mixture among the wraps, top with guacamole and sour cream and roll up.
4. Cut in half and serve hot.

Air Fryer Easy Crispy Chilli Beef

The air fryer is brilliant for making foods with crispy textures, so this takeaway-inspired recipe works a treat.

Servings: 4   Cooking Time: 10 to 30 Mins.

Ingredients:

- 4 x 150g/5½oz minute beef steaks, very thinly sliced into strips
- 1 tbsp soy sauce
- 2 peppers, red or yellow, seeds removed and cut into chunks
- 2 onions, cut into 2cm/¾in chunks
- 1 red chilli, seeds removed, sliced
- 1½ tbsp vegetable oil
- 3 tbsp cornflour
- 2 tsp Chinese five-spice powder
- 2 spring onions, sliced on an angle, to serve
- freshly cooked rice or noodles, to serve (optional)
- For the glaze
- 2 tbsp sesame seeds (a mix of black and white, or whatever you have)
- 5 tbsp white wine vinegar
- 1 tbsp balsamic vinegar
- 2 tbsp light soy sauce
- 2 tbsp light brown sugar
- 2 tbsp tomato ketchup

Directions:

1. Mix the beef strips with the soy sauce in a bowl. Set aside to marinate for 10 minutes.
2. Heat the air fryer to 190C. Toss the pepper, onion and chilli in ½ tablespoon vegetable oil and cook for 10 minutes.
3. To make the glaze, set aside about a teaspoon of the sesame seeds for sprinkling. Mix the remaining seeds with all the glaze ingredients in a small bowl. Pour over the vegetables and return to the air fryer for 2 minutes. Remove and set aside in a bowl.
4. Heat the air fryer to 200C. Add the cornflour, Chinese five-spice and remaining vegetable oil to the marinated beef mixture and mix well to coat. Lay the coated beef slices in the air fryer in a single layer, with space around them for the air to circulate. You may need to do this in two batches.
5. Cook for 7 minutes until the beef strips have crisped up. Remove the tray halfway through and shake so that the beef pieces cook evenly.
6. Once all the beef is cooked, pop the pepper and onion back in the air fryer for 2 minutes to heat up, then remove and mix with the crispy beef. Top with the spring onions and reserved sesame seeds and serve with rice or noodles, if using.

Notes:

1. This recipe will work well with chicken too.
2. To prepare this dish ahead of time, marinate the beef up to 3 hours in advance. The vegetables can be cooked the day before.
3. The beef is best eaten just after cooking.

Air Fryer Chicken Strips

Southern-style flour dredged chicken strips are easy to make in the air fryer and make a great alternative to breaded chicken tenders. Serve with a creamy American-style honey mustard dipping sauce.

Servings: 2   Cooking Time: 10 to 30 Mins.

Ingredients:

- 2 large garlic cloves, minced or crushed
- 5 tbsp plain yoghurt
- ¼ tsp salt, plus extra for seasoning
- 2 chicken breasts
- 6 tbsp plain flour
- 6 tbsp panko breadcrumbs
- 1 tsp sweet smoked paprika
- 1 tsp garlic granules
- ½ tsp cayenne pepper
- freshly ground black pepper
- 1 free-range egg
- olive oil cooking spray
- For the creamy honey mustard dip
- 1 tbsp runny honey
- 1 tbsp light mayonnaise
- 1 tbsp Dijon mustard
- ½ tbsp wholegrain mustard
- ½ tsp white wine vinegar

Directions:

1. To marinate the chicken, combine the garlic with the yoghurt and salt. Cut the chicken into roughly 3cm/1¼in wide strips and marinate in the yoghurt mixture for at least 20 minutes, or overnight.
2. In a medium bowl combine the flour, breadcrumbs, paprika, garlic granules, cayenne pepper and a generous amount of salt and pepper to create the dredging mixture. In another small bowl, beat the egg and season with salt and pepper.
3. Shake off any excess yoghurt from each chicken strip before dipping it first in the egg, then in the dredging mixture. Use one hand for wet ingredients and another for dry to avoid coating your fingers!
4. Spray the bottom of the air fryer basket with olive oil spray and arrange a single layer of chicken strips in the bottom. Spray the top of the chicken strips with oil before air-frying for 15 minutes at 200C, turning roughly halfway through. Repeat until all the chicken strips are cooked (you will need to work in batches).
5. Meanwhile, combine all the ingredients for the creamy honey mustard dip in a small bowl, and set aside. When all the chicken is cooked, serve alongside the dip.

Notes:

1. This recipe was tested working in two batches in a 3.2 litre/5½ pint basket air fryer, but it is not suited to a model fitted with a stirring paddle. It is also easily scaled up in a larger air fryer.

Air Fryer Meatballs With Cherry Tomato Sauce

In this easy family supper both the meatballs and sauce are made in the air fryer, creating delicious results while saving you time and energy.

Servings: 4   Cooking Time: 30 Mins. to 1 Hour

Ingredients:

- For the beef meatballs
- 80g/2¾oz breadcrumbs
- 2 tbsp milk
- 1 medium free-range egg
- 500g/1lb 2oz beef mince
- 2 tbsp finely chopped fresh parsley
- 2 tbsp finely chopped fresh basil
- 100g/3½oz feta
- For the sauce
- 2 garlic cloves, peeled and cut in half
- 400g/14oz cherry tomatoes, cut in half lengthways
- 1 medium shallot, finely chopped (approx. 50g/1¾oz)
- 1 tbsp olive oil
- 1 tbsp balsamic vinegar
- salt and freshly ground black pepper
- To serve
- 400g/14oz dried spaghetti
- 2 tbsp butter
- 1 tbsp roughly chopped fresh parsley
- 1 tbsp roughly chopped fresh basil
- 50g/1¾oz feta, crumbled

Directions:

1. To make the meatballs, mix together the breadcrumbs, milk and egg in a large bowl. Add the beef, parsley and basil then crumble in the feta. Season with salt and pepper and mix well before shaping into 16 balls.
2. Preheat the air fryer to 200C. Pull out the basket and line with an air fryer paper tray, or use baking paper to form a low-sided base.
3. To make the sauce, place the garlic, cherry tomatoes and shallots on the lined tray. Season with salt and pepper, then drizzle with the olive oil and balsamic vinegar.
4. Air fry for 25 minutes, shaking the vegetables at the halfway point.
5. Once cooked, carefully tip the vegetables into a large bowl, discard the paper then use a stick blender to blend until smooth. Alternatively, blend in a food processor. Transfer the sauce to a small pan and keep warm over a low heat; leave the air fryer on.
6. Place the meatballs into the air fryer, spacing them out evenly, and cook for 10–12 minutes or until cooked through.
7. Meanwhile, cook the spaghetti according to packet instructions. Drain and stir through the butter.
8. To serve, pile the spaghetti onto a plate and top with the meatballs and sauce. Garnish with a sprinkle of chopped parsley, basil and a little crumbled feta.

Notes:

1. If making the meatballs ahead, place on a tray lined with baking paper and chill in the fridge until needed.

Air Fryer Beef Tacos

The air fryer is just the thing to quickly cook strips of steak for this beef taco recipe, served with a tomato and chilli dressing. Feel free to riff on the herbs - basil is great, but you might be a fan of the traditional coriander. It makes 8 tacos, so it's ideal for sharing.

Servings: 8   **Cooking Time: 10 to 30 Mins.**

Ingredients:
- 500g/1lb 2oz rump or sirloin steak, cut into strips or small chunks
- 1 tsp vegetable oil
- 1 tbsp Cajun seasoning
- 1 lime, juice only
- 8 small soft tortilla wraps
- lime wedges, to serve
- pomegranate seeds, to serve (optional)
- For the tomato and basil dressing
- handful fresh basil
- 3 tbsp olive oil
- 2 garlic cloves, crushed
- 1 red chilli, seeds removed, chopped
- handful cherry tomatoes, finely chopped
- salt and freshly ground black pepper

Directions:
1. Preheat the air fryer to 200C.
2. Coat the steak in the oil, Cajun seasoning and lime juice. Air-fry the steak for 6 minutes then shake the air fryer basket and cook for a further 2 minutes.
3. Meanwhile, to make the dressing, combine all the ingredients in a bowl.
4. Wrap the tortillas in foil and add to the air fryer for 2 minutes to warm through. Alternatively, char them over a gas hob.
5. Add the steak to the tortillas and top with the dressing. Serve with lime wedges to squeeze over. If you like, sprinkle over some pomegranate seeds for a fresh, juicy contrast.

Air Fryer Sausage Rolls With Black Pudding

Servings: 8-10 **Cooking Time: 10 to 30 Mins.**

Ingredients:

- 300g/10½oz sausagemeat or sausages with skins removed
- ½ tsp mustard powder
- ½ tsp dried sage
- ½ tsp dried thyme
- 100g/3½oz black pudding, casing removed, roughly chopped
- 1 sheet (320g) ready-rolled puff pastry
- 1 free-range egg, beaten
- your favourite dipping sauce, to serve

Directions:

1. Using a fork, mix together the sausagemeat, mustard powder, herbs and black pudding. Using your hands, mould the mixture into two long sausage shapes.
2. Cut the pastry in half lengthways.
3. Lay the meat mixture along the centre of each piece of pastry.
4. Brush the edges with beaten egg, then fold the pastry over the filling and crimp the edges with a fork to seal. Cut into sausage rolls, to the size you prefer.
5. Brush over the sausage rolls with beaten egg, then air-fry at 200C for 12–14 minutes until golden brown.
6. Serve hot or cold, with your favourite dipping sauce.

Air Fryer Pork Chops

Peppered pork chops make a wonderfully tasty midweek meal, coated in a mix of savoury seasonings and crushed peppercorns. It's super-quick to cook in the air fryer. Gorgeous with couscous, corn on the cob and some leafy green salad.

Servings: 4　　Cooking Time: 10 to 30 Mins.

Ingredients:

- 4 pork chops
- 1–2 tbsp vegetable oil or a few sprays of low-calorie cooking oil spray
- 1 tbsp paprika
- 1 tsp American burger seasoning
- 1 tsp onion granules
- 1 tsp garlic granules
- 1 tsp dried parsley
- 1 tsp crushed peppercorns
- salt
- couscous, corn on the cob and salad, to serve

Directions:

1. Preheat the air fryer to 200C.
2. Dry the chops with kitchen paper then put them in a bowl and coat in the oil. Add all the seasonings and mix well to coat.
3. Cook in the air fryer for 10–12 minutes, or 14 minutes if the chops are extra-large.
4. Serve with couscous, corn on the cob and salad.

Air Fryer Mozzarella Sticks

The key to creating restaurant-style, crispy, breadcrumbed mozzarella sticks in the air fryer is to cook them from frozen: give them at least 30 minutes in the freezer. They're delicious served with a spicy tomato ketchup.

Servings: 3-4 **Cooking Time: 10 to 30 Mins.**

Ingredients:
- 400g block mozzarella cucina
- 2 tbsp plain flour
- 1 tsp garlic granules
- 1 large free-range egg
- 40g/1½oz panko breadcrumbs
- olive oil cooking spray
- salt and freshly ground black pepper

Directions:
1. Cut the mozzarella into strips, roughly 1.5cm/⅝in wide, and pat dry using kitchen paper.
2. In a shallow dish, mix together the flour and the garlic granules. In another dish, beat the egg with a generous amount of salt and pepper. Spread the breadcrumbs in a third dish.
3. Roll the mozzarella strips in flour, then in egg, then in flour and egg again, to create a double coating. Make sure each piece is totally covered in flour each time; any gaps will cause the mozzarella sticks to leak in the air fryer. Coat well in the panko breadcrumbs.
4. Freeze for at least 30 minutes until solid.
5. Spray the bottom of the air fryer basket with olive oil spray and arrange a single layer of mozzarella sticks in the bottom. Spray the top of the mozzarella sticks with oil before air-frying for 10 minutes at 200C. Repeat until all the mozzarella sticks are cooked, keeping each batch warm, then serve immediately.

Notes:
1. Mozzarella cucina is a firm, low-moisture cooking mozzarella sold in a block. Often labelled as ideal for pizza, it is shrink-wrapped rather than packed in whey.
2. This recipe was tested working in two batches in a 3.2 litre/5½ pint basket air fryer; in a larger air fryer the sticks can be cooked in one batch. It is not suited to a model fitted with a stirring paddle.

Air Fryer Blueberry Baked Oats

These air fryer blueberry baked oats give the illusion of eating cake for breakfast! The whole family will be begging you to make them every morning.

Servings: 4

Cooking Time: 10 to 30 Mins.

Ingredients:

- 2 free-range eggs
- 400ml/14fl oz milk
- 4 tbsp runny honey or maple syrup
- 200g/7oz porridge oats
- 2 tsp baking powder
- large pinch salt
- 100g/3½oz fresh blueberries or any frozen berries
- plain yoghurt, to serve (optional)

Directions:

1. Beat together the eggs, milk and honey in a large bowl. Add the oats, baking powder and salt to the bowl, stirring until well mixed. If you have time, leave to sit for 5–10 minutes so the oats can soak up the milk. Preheat the air fryer to 175C.
2. Divide the mixture between four small heatproof dishes or 150ml/5fl oz ramekins and then scatter over the blueberries.
3. Air fry for 10–12 minutes until golden and set. Serve warm or chilled, topped with a spoonful of yoghurt, if using.

Notes:

1. Make the mixture the night before and store covered in the fridge to make breakfast even faster in the morning. Remove from the fridge to allow to come to room temperature before topping with blueberries and cooking.
2. If you don't have an air fryer you can bake these in an oven preheated to 200C/180C Fan/Gas 6 for 20-25 minutes.

Air Fryer Baked Eggs

Quick and easy, these baked eggs make a delicious breakfast or brunch served with a side of buttered toast soldiers. Enjoy as they are or get creative with a variety of toppings.

Servings: 4 **Cooking Time: 10 to 30 Mins.**

Ingredients:
- 2 tsp softened butter, for greasing
- 4 medium free-range eggs
- 4 tbsp double cream
- salt and freshly ground black pepper
- For the tomato, bacon and cheese topping
- 4 cherry tomatoes, cut into quarters
- 2 rashers cooked smoked streaky bacon, cut into small pieces
- 4 tsp grated cheddar
- For the spinach, black olive and feta topping
- 12 leaves baby spinach, finely shredded
- 8 black olives, de-stoned and roughly chopped
- 4 tbsp crumbled feta
- For the yoghurt, pepper and chilli topping
- 4 tbsp Greek-style or natural yoghurt
- 4 tbsp finely chopped pepper (any colour)
- 4 pinches dried red chilli flakes
- 4 pinches ground cumin
- 1 tsp finely shredded fresh parsley, to be sprinkled after cooking

Directions:
1. Preheat the air fryer to 150C. Lightly grease the inside of four 120ml/4oz ramekins with the butter.
2. Crack an egg into each ramekin, making sure the yolk stays whole. Spoon 1 tablespoon of cream over the egg white – it doesn't matter if it spreads a little onto the yolk.
3. If using a topping, add your chosen ingredients now, dividing the quantities listed above equally between the four ramekins. Each topping recipe is enough for four eggs.
4. For the basic eggs, bake in the air fryer for 7–10 minutes, or until the whites are just set and the yolk is cooked to your liking. For eggs with added toppings, bake for 12–15 minutes.
5. Season with salt and freshly ground black pepper to serve.

Air Fryer Chicken Thighs With Honey, Chilli And Soy Glaze

These sweet and sticky chicken thighs are packed with flavour and simple to make. Best of all, this meal won't leave you with stacks of washing up.

Servings: 4 **Cooking Time: 10 to 30 Mins.**

Ingredients:
- 2 tbsp runny honey
- 4 tbsp soy sauce
- 1 lime, zest and juice
- 2 tbsp sesame oil
- pinch chilli flakes
- 20g/2/3 oz fresh root ginger, peeled and grated
- 8 chicken thighs, skin on, bone in
- 40g/1½oz salted butter, diced
- salt and freshly ground black pepper
- To serve
- 2 spring onions, finely sliced
- 2 tsp sesame seeds
- 10g/1/3 oz fresh coriander, stalks finely chopped, leaves roughly chopped

Directions:
1. To make the marinade, whisk together the honey, soy sauce, lime zest and juice, sesame oil, chilli flakes and ginger in a large bowl. Pour half the mixture into a small saucepan and set aside.
2. Add the chicken to the bowl, stirring to make sure the meat is well covered with the marinade and season well with salt and pepper. Chill in the fridge for 30 minutes.
3. Preheat the air fryer to 200C.
4. Place the chicken thighs skin-side down in the air fryer basket, spreading them out so they don't quite touch. You may need to cook them in two batches depending on the size of your air fryer. Air fry for 22–25 minutes or until cooked through, turning them skin-side up after 10 minutes.
5. Once cooked, remove the chicken from the basket and onto your serving plates.
6. To make the glaze, bring the remaining marinade to the boil on the hob, then immediately remove from the heat and whisk in the butter.
7. Drizzle the glaze over the chicken thighs and top with the sliced spring onions, sesame seeds and fresh coriander to serve.

Air Fryer Sausage Bake

This air fryer sausage bake is a super speedy all-in-one meal, perfect for weeknights when you're low on time and energy.

Servings: 4   **Cooking Time: 30 Mins. to 1 Hour**

Ingredients:
- 1 red onion, quartered, or 1 leek, cut into pieces
- 1 red pepper, seeds removed and cut into chunks
- 180g/6¼oz cherry tomatoes
- 1 courgette, cut into 2cm/¾in chunks
- olive oil spray
- 150ml/5fl oz chicken stock
- 2 tbsp tomato purée
- 4 medium potatoes (about 400g/14oz in total), scrubbed and sliced into 1cm/½in thick wedges
- 8 pork sausages
- handful basil leaves, to garnish (optional)

Directions:
1. Heat the air fryer to 190C. Place the onion, pepper, cherry tomatoes and courgette in a container that will fit in the air fryer (see Recipe Tip) and spray with olive oil.
2. Roast for 10 minutes, then mix together the stock and tomato purée in a jug and pour this over the vegetables. Return to the air fryer for 5 minutes then set aside.
3. Toss the potato wedges in a few sprays of olive oil. Place in a lined basket of the air fryer and cook for 12 minutes. Remove and shake the pan or turn the potatoes, then top with the sausages. Cook for 10 minutes or until done, turning after 6 minutes. (If the air fryer basket is smaller, do this in two batches.)
4. Combine the vegetables and the sausage mixture and return to the air fryer for 2 minutes to heat through. Spoon the sausage bake into a serving dish and top with the basil leaves, if using. Serve immediately.

Notes:
1. If it fits, use a 20cm/8in round cake tin to bake everything in – it works a treat when adding the liquids too. Just make sure it's not a loose-bottomed tin!
2. Feel free to swap in vegetarian sausages for a veggie version.

Air Fryer Salmon With Warm Potato Salad

A honey and mustard glaze complements both the salmon and the warm potato salad. To serve the salmon with other sides, simply halve the glaze quantity.

Servings: 4   **Cooking Time: 10 to 30 Mins.**

Ingredients:

- 500g/1lb 2oz small new potatoes, larger ones halved
- 4 salmon fillets, approx. 150g/5½oz each, scaled
- 250g/9oz green beans (or thin-stemmed broccoli), trimmed
- 250g/9oz sugar snap peas (or mangetout)
- 1 long or 2 round shallots, finely chopped
- 2 tbsp white wine vinegar
- salt and freshly ground black pepper
- For the glaze
- 3 tbsp runny honey
- 3 tbsp wholegrain mustard

Directions:

1. Half-fill a large saucepan with water and bring to the boil. Preheat the air fryer to 200C.
2. Meanwhile, for the glaze, mix together the honey and mustard in a medium–large mixing bowl. Transfer half the glaze to a smaller container and season.
3. When the water is boiling, add the potatoes and cook for 7 minutes.
4. Line the air fryer basket with a piece of baking paper that covers the bottom and comes 2–4cm/about 1–1½in up the sides. Put the salmon, skin-side down, on the paper and brush the fillets with the seasoned honey-mustard glaze. (If you need to cook the salmon in two batches, use half the seasoned glaze per batch.) Air-fry for 6 minutes, then use a fork to check if the fish flakes in the thickest part; if not, cook for 1 minute more, or until cooked through.
5. When the potatoes have been boiling for 7 minutes, add the green beans and sugar snap peas and cook for a further 3–4 minutes, until everything is tender. If using mangetout, add only for the last 2 minutes of cooking time.
6. Drain the vegetables well. Stir the shallot, vinegar and some seasoning into the reserved honey-mustard glaze. Tip in the hot vegetables and gently stir to coat in the dressing.
7. Use the baking paper to help you lift the salmon from the air fryer and serve with the warm potato and vegetable salad.

Notes:

1. If you have a steamer basket, boil the potatoes in a pan for 10 minutes, then put the beans and sugar snaps in the basket above the boiling water and steam for the final 4 minutes. If using mangetout, steam for 2 minutes only.
2. For a romantic dinner for two, simply halve all the ingredients.

Air Fryer Crispy Tofu

Cooking crispy tofu in an air fryer is a game changer. Perfect results every time! Make these crispy tofu bites the star of your next party.

Servings: 4 **Cooking Time: 10 to 30 Mins.**

Ingredients:
- 280g/10oz extra firm tofu, drained
- 1 tbsp soy sauce
- 1 tbsp vegetable oil
- 1 garlic clove, crushed or grated
- 1 tsp grated fresh root ginger
- 1 tsp paprika
- pinch salt
- 2 tbsp cornflour
- sweet chilli sauce, to serve

Directions:
1. Pat the tofu dry with kitchen paper and cut into 20–25 cubes. Preheat the air fryer to 200C.
2. Mix the soy sauce, oil, garlic, ginger, paprika and salt together in a bowl. Stir the tofu cubes into the soy mixture and then sprinkle in the cornflour, stirring gently until evenly coated.
3. Air fry for 12–15 minutes, shaking halfway through, until crisp and golden. Serve immediately with the chilli sauce for dipping.

Notes:
1. If you don't have an air fryer you can cook these in a regular oven preheated to 220C/200C Fan/Gas 7 for 25 minutes.

Air Fryer Beef Tacos

The air fryer is just the thing to quickly cook strips of steak for this beef taco recipe, served with a tomato and chilli dressing. Feel free to riff on the herbs - basil is great, but you might be a fan of the traditional coriander. It makes 8 tacos, so it's ideal for sharing.

Servings: 8   **Cooking Time: 10 to 30 Mins.**

Ingredients:

- 500g/1lb 2oz rump or sirloin steak, cut into strips or small chunks
- 1 tsp vegetable oil
- 1 tbsp Cajun seasoning
- 1 lime, juice only
- 8 small soft tortilla wraps
- lime wedges, to serve
- pomegranate seeds, to serve (optional)
- For the tomato and basil dressing
- handful fresh basil
- 3 tbsp olive oil
- 2 garlic cloves, crushed
- 1 red chilli, seeds removed, chopped
- handful cherry tomatoes, finely chopped
- salt and freshly ground black pepper

Directions:

1. Preheat the air fryer to 200C.
2. Coat the steak in the oil, Cajun seasoning and lime juice. Air-fry the steak for 6 minutes then shake the air fryer basket and cook for a further 2 minutes.
3. Meanwhile, to make the dressing, combine all the ingredients in a bowl.
4. Wrap the tortillas in foil and add to the air fryer for 2 minutes to warm through. Alternatively, char them over a gas hob.
5. Add the steak to the tortillas and top with the dressing. Serve with lime wedges to squeeze over. If you like, sprinkle over some pomegranate seeds for a fresh, juicy contrast.

Air Fryer Pork Steak Sandwich

Step aside pulled pork, here's a crispy alternative. This air fryer pork steak sandwich is just as great in a bun and ready in no time at all.

Servings: 2   Cooking Time: 10 to 30 Mins.

Ingredients:
- For the quick pickled onions
- ½ red onion, sliced into 1cm/¾in rings
- 1 tbsp white vinegar or lemon juice
- 1 tsp caster sugar
- For the pork sandwiches
- 2 tbsp plain flour
- 1 free-range large egg, beaten
- 50g/1¾oz panko breadcrumbs
- 2 pork loin steaks (about 150–200g/5½–7oz each)
- olive oil spray, for frying
- 1 small green or red apple, cored and sliced into 1cm/¾in rounds
- salt and freshly ground black pepper
- chopped lettuce, to serve (optional)
- 2 burger buns or bread rolls, split, to serve
- mayonnaise, to serve (optional)

Directions:
1. To make the pickled onions, mix the onion, vinegar and caster sugar together in a small bowl. Set aside to pickle.
2. Heat the air fryer to 200C. To make the sandwiches, spread the flour out on a large plate and season well with salt and pepper. Place the egg in a bowl and spread the breadcrumbs out on another large plate.
3. Dip a pork steak in the flour, then the egg, and finally the breadcrumbs. Double dip on the top and bottom of the pork steak for a thicker, crispy coating. Repeat with the other steak.
4. Spray the steaks a few times with the oil spray, then lay the two steaks on the rack in the air fryer and place half of the apple slices around them.
5. Cook for 5 minutes, then flip the steaks (if the apple slices are cooked by this point, remove and set aside until serving). Cook for another 4–8 minutes on the other side, depending on the thickness of the pork. It should take a total of 12 minutes for a 3cm/1¼in thick piece of pork and approximately 8 minutes for a 2cm/¾in thick piece of pork.
6. To serve, place some lettuce, if using, in the buns, then layer with slices of the steak or whole pork steaks. Top with the pickled onion, roasted apple slices and the mayonnaise, if using. Serve immediately.

Notes:
1. If you have time, mix together 250ml/9fl oz cider with 1 tablespoon Dijon mustard in a large bowl. Add the pork steaks and marinate in the mustard mixture overnight or for a few hours. Once marinated, follow the recipe as detailed here.
2. This recipe was developed using a 5.5 litre/9½ pint air fryer.

Air Fryer Tomato, Pepper And Feta Pasta

A versatile air fryer pasta dish that is full of flavour and goodness, with fresh tomatoes, red pepper, feta and olives. It's perfect for any type of fresh pasta, filled pasta or gnocchi.

Servings: 2 **Cooking Time: 10 to 30 Mins.**

Ingredients:

- 600g/1lb 5oz vine-ripened tomatoes, roughly chopped
- 1 red pepper, seeds removed, roughly chopped
- 4 fresh bay leaves
- 2 sprigs fresh rosemary, leaves chopped
- 1 tbsp sun-dried tomato paste
- 3 tbsp extra virgin olive oil
- 1 vegetable or chicken stock cube, crumbled
- 1 tsp smoked paprika
- 250g/9oz fresh pasta
- 80g/2¾oz pitted Kalamata olives, halved
- 80g/2¾oz feta, crumbled
- 2 tbsp fresh flatleaf parsley, roughly chopped
- salt and freshly ground black pepper

Directions:

1. Preheat the air fryer to 180C.
2. Put the tomatoes, red pepper, bay leaves, rosemary, sun-dried tomato paste, olive oil, stock cube and paprika into a heatproof dish that fits into your air fryer.
3. Season with salt and pepper and cook for 15 minutes, stirring twice.
4. Carefully remove the dish from the air fryer. Discard the bay leaves and then, using a stick blender, blitz until smooth.
5. Put the dish back into the air fryer and spoon in the pasta, stirring to ensure it is well coated in the sauce. Cook for a further 8 minutes.
6. Scatter over the olives, feta and parsley and mix well. Grind over plenty of black pepper and serve.

Notes:

1. This sauce goes well with breaded chicken or fish, instead of the pasta.
2. If you like, swap the paprika for chilli or the olives for capers.
3. For extra veggies, grate in some fresh courgettes.

Air Fryer Sweet Potato And Chorizo Hash

A speedy lunch or an incredible breakfast, brunch or supper from the air fryer. Sweet potato goes so well with smoky chorizo – add a spoonful of yoghurt and a drizzle of garlic chilli butter and you're in heaven.

Servings: 3-4   **Cooking Time: 10 to 30 Mins.**

Ingredients:

- 600g/1lb 7oz sweet potatoes, peeled and cubed
- 1 tbsp vegetable oil or a few sprays of low-calorie cooking oil spray
- 1 tbsp paprika
- 150g/5½oz chorizo, sliced
- 1 tbsp light or half-fat butter
- 1 garlic clove, grated
- ½ tsp dried chilli flakes
- 4 tbsp Greek-style yoghurt
- 1–2 tbsp freshly chopped dill
- salt and freshly ground black pepper
- To serve (optional)
- toasted sourdough bread
- poached eggs
- mashed avocado

Directions:

1. Mix the sweet potatoes with the oil and paprika.
2. Air fry at 190C for 14–15 minutes; add the chorizo after about 12 minutes.
3. While the chorizo is cooking, melt the butter with the garlic and chilli in the microwave for 1 minute.
4. Season the yoghurt with salt and pepper.
5. To serve, spoon the yoghurt over the sweet potatoes, top with the garlic chilli butter and sprinkle with dill.
6. If you like, serve with toasted sourdough, poached eggs or mashed avocado.

Air Fryer Pizza

These pizzas are super quick to put together, whether you make our speedy no-prove dough or use a naan or flatbread as a base. Ideal as a WFH lunch or speedy dinner on busy weeknights.

Servings: 4   Cooking Time: 30 Mins. to 1 Hour

Ingredients:
- 400g tin plum tomatoes
- 300g/10½oz self-raising flour, plus extra for dusting
- 1 tsp baking powder
- ½ tsp salt
- 300g/10½oz plain yoghurt
- 4 sprays olive oil spray
- toppings of your choice, such as olives, sliced red onion, artichoke or ham (optional)
- 200g/7oz firm mozzarella cheese, grated
- rocket leaves, to serve (optional)

Directions:
1. Empty the tomatoes into a sieve over a bowl and squish them with a spoon or your hands to break them up slightly. Set aside to drain for 10 minutes. (The drained juice can be used for another recipe – see Recipe Tip.) Set aside the drained tomatoes in a bowl.
2. Meanwhile, mix together the flour, baking powder and salt in a bowl. Add the yoghurt and mix with a knife or your hands to form a soft dough. Divide into four pieces.
3. Roll each piece out on a well-floured surface to a circle that fits in the air fryer (this will be around 20cm/8in in diameter for a 5.5 litre/9½ pint single basket air fryer).
4. Preheat the air fryer to 205C. Lay one pizza base on the rack of the air fryer and spray with olive oil spray once, then prick with a fork a few times. Cook for 3 minutes. Remove, flip over and return to the air-fryer for another 2 minutes.
5. Take out the basket, place on a wooden board and spread a quarter of the drained tomatoes over the pizza. Add your choice of toppings, followed by a quarter of the mozzarella. Any toppings that need to cook (such as onion slices) should go on top of the cheese so that they meet the heat first.
6. Cook for 4 minutes until the cheese is bubbling and the base is crispy. Remove and repeat with the remaining pizzas. Top each pizza with rocket leaves (if using) and serve.

Notes:
1. Use firm mozzarella cheese as mozzarella balls retain a lot of moisture. However, if you have time, you can drain fresh mozzarella balls by leaving to soak on kitchen paper, covered in the fridge, for a few hours or overnight.
2. Use the drained tomato juice for a quick Bloody Mary, or add to any soups or stews.
3. Use naan breads or flatbreads as bases instead of making the pizza dough. Just ignore the steps on making and cooking the base and proceed with the pizza topping.
4. This recipe was developed using a 5.5 litre/9½ pint air fryer.

Air Fryer Sweet Potato Fries

These crispy air fryer sweet potato fries have less fat and more vitamins than regular potato fries. Great with vegan and vegetarian bakes and burgers, or with chicken or fish dishes.

Servings: 2   **Cooking Time: 10 to 30 Mins.**

Ingredients:
- 325–350g/11½–12oz small–medium sweet potatoes, scrubbed clean
- 2 tsp light rapeseed, sunflower or vegetable oil
- ¼ tsp dried oregano
- ¼ tsp paprika or smoked paprika, plus a pinch to serve (optional)
- salt and freshly ground black pepper

Directions:
1. Preheat the air fryer to 200C. Cut the sweet potatoes into 1cm/½in thick chips: try to cut evenly to ensure even cooking and crispness, and keep in mind that shorter chips are easier to fit into the air fryer.
2. Tip the chips into a bowl, drizzle over the oil and sprinkle with the dried oregano and paprika, if using. Season with salt – it will help the fries crisp up – and pepper.
3. Put a single layer of chips in the base of the air fryer – don't overcrowd or they won't cook evenly. Air-fry for 8 minutes, using tongs to turn them halfway through, until golden and crisp on the outside, and soft on the inside. If they're not quite done, continue to cook for a minute at a time before checking again.
4. Cook in two or three batches until all the fries are ready, then put them all back into the air fryer to heat through for 30 seconds. Serve immediately, sprinkled with more seasoning and a pinch more paprika, if using.

Notes:
1. If you find your fries aren't crisp enough, try cutting them more finely the next time you make them.
2. If your oven is on for something else, you can keep the first batches of fries warm while you air-fry the rest.
3. If your air fryer is fitted with a stirring paddle, you won't need to turn the fries during cooking.

Air Fryer Roast Potatoes

If you're looking for a lighter, healthier version of a roast potato, or you're simply short on oven space, try this air fryer roast potato recipe for delicious, crisp on the outside, fluffy on the inside, roast potatoes!

Servings: 2 **Cooking Time: 30 Mins. to 1 Hour**

Ingredients:

- 2 large floury potatoes (approximately 450g/1lb) (see Recipe Tip)
- salt, to taste
- 1 tbsp olive oil

Directions:

1. Peel and quarter the potatoes before par-boiling them in a saucepan of already boiling, salted water for 15 minutes.
2. Drain the potatoes well and leave them to steam dry for a minute or two before tossing with the olive oil and a generous seasoning of salt.
3. Air-fry for 30 minutes at 200C, tossing every 10 minutes to ensure they crisp up and brown evenly.

Notes:

1. This recipe was tested in a 3.2 litre/5½ pint basket air fryer. It will also work in a model fitted with a stirring paddle – in this case, you will not need to toss the potatoes during cooking. It is also easily scaled up to feed more people in a larger air fryer.
2. Large potatoes are best for this recipe, if you are using smaller potatoes make sure they are cut into large chunks or reduce the par-boil time.

Air Fryer Sausage And Bean Casserole

An all-in-one sausage and bean casserole, cooked in the air fryer for an easy midweek dinner for two. It's packed with veggies, so you don't need anything else with this, but some warm focaccia or ciabatta drizzled with extra virgin olive oil would be a lovely accompaniment.

Servings: 2   **Cooking Time:** 30 Mins. to 1 Hour

Ingredients:

- 4 good-quality sausages
- 3½ tbsp extra virgin olive oil
- 1 onion, sliced into half moons
- 2 celery sticks, finely sliced
- 2 carrots, peeled and chopped into 2cm/¾in cubes
- 3 bay leaves
- 1 tbsp finely chopped fresh sage, plus a few leaves to serve
- 1 sprig fresh rosemary, leaves finely chopped
- 400g tin chopped tomatoes
- 1 tbsp sun-dried tomato paste
- 1 chicken stock cube
- 400g tin borlotti or cannellini beans, drained and rinsed
- 50g/1¾oz cavolo nero, stalks removed, leaves shredded
- 15g/½oz pecorino, finely grated
- salt and freshly ground black pepper

Directions:

1. Preheat the air fryer to 180C.
2. Line the air fryer basket with kitchen foil, add the sausages and drizzle with ½ tablespoon olive oil. Cook for 8 minutes, turning halfway through.
3. Remove the sausages and set aside.
4. Put the onion, celery, carrots, herbs, 3 tablespoons olive oil and some salt and pepper into a heatproof dish that fits into your air fryer and cook for 5 minutes.
5. Add the tomatoes, tomato paste, stock cube, 300ml/½ pint water and the sausages and cook for 15 minutes.
6. Add the beans and cavolo nero and stir through; cook for a further 5 minutes.
7. Discard the bay leaves.
8. You can slice the sausages at an angle or keep them whole. Serve topped with a few sage leaves and some grated pecorino.

Notes:

1. If you are struggling to find a heatproof dish that fits in your air fryer, you could use a fixed-base cake tin about 18cm/7in in diameter.
2. You can swap the borlotti for any other beans, and use your favourite sausages.

Air Fryer Baked Potato

Air fryers are more energy-efficient than ovens and baked potatoes cook in about half the usual time. Air-frying also gives a crispy skin and creamy middle, perfect with any of these three delicious toppings.

Servings: 1 **Cooking Time:** 30 Mins. to 1 Hour

Ingredients:

- 1 baking potato (see recipe tips and weigh before cooking), scrubbed and dried
- light rapeseed, vegetable or sunflower oil
- salt and freshly ground black pepper
- For the cheddar and jalapeño topping
- small handful grated cheddar
- 1 ripe tomato, diced
- few green jalapeño pepper slices from a jar
- For the smashed avocado topping
- 1 small, ripe avocado (or a few frozen avocado slices)
- ½ lime or lemon, juice only
- handful mixed seeds, dukkah, za'atar or chilli flakes
- For the curried beans topping
- 227g tin baked beans
- ½ tsp curry powder
- natural yoghurt and lime pickle (optional), to serve

Directions:

1. Rub the potato all over with a little oil. If you like, rub a little salt over the skin – this will help give a crispier finish.
2. Put the potato in the air fryer and turn to 200C (you don't want to preheat, to avoid burning the skin before the inside is cooked.) Air-fry for 20 minutes, then turn the potato over. A small potato will take another 20 minutes or so, a large one another 25–30 minutes.
3. Check the middle is soft by poking a table knife into the centre – it should slide in easily. If it's not quite done, continue to cook for a minute at a time.
4. For the cheddar and jalapeño topping, mix the cheese, tomato and jalapeño slices, split the potato and spoon the cheese mixture on top.
5. For the smashed avocado topping, mash the avocado with the lime or lemon juice, salt and pepper. Split the potato, spoon in the avocado mixture and scatter with the seeds or your choice of seasoning.
6. For the curried beans topping, heat the beans with the curry powder until hot but not boiling. Split the potato and pile on the beans. Top with dollops of yoghurt and lime pickle, if using.

Notes:

1. Small potatoes, around 225g/8oz each, will be ready in 40 minutes. Large potatoes, around 350g/12oz each, will take 45–50 minutes to get soft inside.
2. You can speed up the cooking by microwaving your jacket potatoes first. Microwave on high power for four minutes, turn the potato over, and microwave for another four minutes. (If you are cooking two potatoes, you may need to microwave them for an extra 2 minutes.) Then cook in the air-fryer for 10 minutes to crisp up.
3. Look for potatoes labelled as bakers, or a floury variety, such as King Edward, Maris Piper, Vivaldi or Estima.

Air Fryer Cauliflower 'Wings'

Delicious right out of the air fryer, these vegan cauliflower 'wings' are crunchy and spicy drizzled with hot sauce. Add the water slowly and ensure you have a really thick batter that clings to the florets so it doesn't drip through the air fryer basket holes.

Servings: 4   Cooking Time: 10 to 30 Mins.

Ingredients:
- 1 small–medium cauliflower, cut the cauliflower into florets, approx. 4–6cm/1½–2½in, save the stalk and leaves for another recipe
- 125g/4½oz plain flour
- 1 tsp baking powder
- 1 tsp paprika
- cooking oil spray
- 2–3 tbsp buffalo hot sauce (check that it's vegan)
- salt and freshly ground black pepper
- For the dip
- 175g/6oz unsweetened oat-based yoghurt
- 1 small garlic clove, crushed or finely grated
- 1 lemon, zest only, plus juice of ½ lemon
- 3 tbsp finely chopped fresh herbs, such as coriander, chives, dill, mint – or a mix

Directions:
1. Preheat the air fryer to 200C.
2. Put the flour, baking powder and paprika in a bowl with some salt and pepper. Whisk in 150ml/¼ pint cold water to make a thick batter. Dip the cauliflower florets in to coat them and set aside on a plate.
3. Spray the air fryer basket with oil, then add the florets in a single layer (they can be touching: you can break them apart after cooking). Spray the tops with more oil and air-fry for 10 minutes, or until golden brown and crispy but cooked through. (You may need to cook in two batches.)
4. Meanwhile, make the dip. Mix the yoghurt, garlic, lemon zest and juice together in a bowl, then stir in the chopped herbs and season to taste.
5. If you cooked the cauliflower in batches, put all the florets back into the air fryer and heat for 1 minute.
6. Put 2 tablespoons of the hot sauce into a big bowl. Tip in the hot cauliflower florets and mix to coat all of the pieces. Serve immediately, drizzled with the third tablespoon of hot sauce if you dare, and the cooling dip alongside.

Notes:
1. This recipe was made in an air fryer without a paddle attachment. The batter needs to set on the cauliflower until it is crisp before it will come away from the air fryer basket.
2. No air fryer? Preheat the oven to 200C/180C Fan/Gas 6. Line a baking sheet with baking paper, spray with cooking oil and bake the battered cauliflower florets for 20 minutes, until crispy.

Air Fryer Chipotle Peppers And Gnocchi

This easy air fryer gnocchi meal produces tender, sweet and slightly charred peppers, and soft, pillowy gnocchi all tossed in a spicy, smoky sauce ready to be loaded up with all your favourite Mexican-inspired toppings. To make this recipe vegan, simply sub out the soured cream for a plant-based alternative.

Servings: 2   Cooking Time: 10 to 30 Mins.

Ingredients:
- 1 tbsp chipotle paste
- 1 tbsp olive oil
- 1 lime, cut in half
- 250g/9oz gnocchi
- 1 red pepper, seeds removed and cut into chunks
- 1 orange or yellow pepper, seeds removed and cut into chunks
- 1 small red onion, cut into chunks
- salt
- To serve
- avocado slices
- soured cream
- tomato salsa

Directions:
1. In a large mixing bowl, whisk together the chipotle paste, olive oil and the juice of one half of the lime to make a paste.
2. Toss the gnocchi, peppers, onion and a generous seasoning of salt in the mixture until everything is well coated. Tip into the air fryer.
3. Air-fry for 15–20 minutes at 200C, stirring every 5 minutes with a spatula to make sure none of the peppers are sticking to the bottom and everything cooks evenly.
4. Serve topped with the avocado, soured cream and tomato salsa. Cut the remaining lime half into wedges and serve alongside.

Notes:
1. This recipe was tested in a 3.2 litre/5½ pint basket air fryer. It will also work in a model fitted with a stirring paddle, and you won't need to toss the veggies during cooking. It is also easily scaled up to suit larger air fryers.

Salmon With Roasted Miso Vegetables

A nutritious, quick and easy dinner for two – roasted potatoes and greens in a miso dressing with pieces of perfectly seasoned pan-fried salmon.

Servings: 2   Cooking Time: 10 to 30 Mins.

Ingredients:
- 300g/10½oz baby new potatoes, halved
- 150g/5½oz green beans, trimmed
- 150g/5½oz Tenderstem broccoli, sliced diagonally
- 2 tsp olive oil
- 2 x 150g/5½oz pieces skinless salmon fillets
- salt and freshly ground black pepper
- lemon wedges, to serve
- For the miso dressing
- 1 tbsp white miso
- 2 tsp olive oil
- 2 tsp white wine vinegar
- ½ tsp toasted sesame oil
- ½ tsp honey
- 1–2 tbsp hot water

Directions:
1. Preheat the oven to 230C/210C Fan/Gas 8 and put a roasting tin on the middle shelf to heat up.
2. Bring a pan of salted water to the boil and add the potatoes. Bring back up to the boil, cook for 6–7 minutes until tender, then drain and leave to steam dry for a couple of minutes.
3. Meanwhile, whisk the dressing ingredients together in a large bowl, adding a little hot water to thin the dressing to a pourable consistency.
4. Tip the potatoes, beans and broccoli into the preheated roasting tin, drizzle with oil and season with salt and pepper. Give everything a good mix, then roast for 10 minutes until the potatoes are soft and the vegetables are beginning to caramelise. Pour the dressing over and toss to coat.
5. Heat a non-stick frying pan over a high heat and season the salmon with a little salt and pepper. Lay the salmon in the pan and cook without moving for 3 minutes. Gently turn the fish over and cook for a further 2 minutes.
6. Serve the salmon with the vegetables and lemon wedges.

Notes:
1. You can cook the potatoes and beans in an air fryer, set to 180C. When the par-boiled potatoes have steam-dried, toss them in some olive oil and add to the air fryer. Cook for 6–8 minutes, then add the beans and the broccoli. Cook for a further 3 minutes until the vegetables are crisped.
2. You can substitute ordinary broccoli and/or cauliflower, cut into florets, for the Tenderstem and beans.

Air Fryer Gnocchi With Pesto Dip

Just three ingredients and 20 minutes are all you need to whip up this super-simple gnocchi recipe, perfect for serving as canapés or at a drinks party. You'll need some cocktail sticks and an air fryer for this recipe.

Servings: 8 **Cooking Time: 10 to 30 Mins.**

Ingredients:

- 2 x 400g packs fresh gnocchi
- 2 tbsp olive oil
- 160g/52/3 oz mayonnaise
- 3 tsp pesto
- salt and freshly ground black pepper

Directions:

1. Preheat the air fryer to 180C. Toss the gnocchi with the oil in a bowl and season well with salt and pepper. Cook in the air fryer for 20 minutes, turning halfway, until crispy and lightly golden.
2. Meanwhile, mix the mayonnaise and pesto together in a small bowl. Serve alongside the gnocchi with some cocktail sticks to skewer the gnocchi for dipping.

Notes:

1. The pesto dip can be changed for all kinds of interesting dipping sauces. Cajun mayo, honey sriracha, smoky BBQ or hot honey mustard are just a few easy throw-together dips for these easy party snacks.
2. You can also cook these in a preheated oven at 200C/180C Fan/Gas 6 for 20 minutes, or until golden-brown all over.

Air Fryer Tofu Nuggets

Light and crispy, these are great veggie alternatives to chicken nuggets. Serve with vegetables for a family-friendly dinner or simply with a dip of your choice as a snack.

Servings: 4 **Cooking Time: 10 to 30 Mins.**

Ingredients:
- For the tofu filling
- 300g/10½oz extra firm tofu
- 2 tbsp light soy sauce
- 1 garlic clove, finely grated
- For the batter
- 150g/5½oz plain flour
- 2 tsp smoked sweet paprika
- 150ml/5fl oz buttermilk
- 1 tbsp apple cider vinegar
- olive oil spray
- salt and freshly ground black pepper
- sweet chilli sauce, to serve (optional)

Directions:
1. To make the filling, drain the tofu on kitchen paper for 10 minutes. Cut into 3cm/1¼in cubes and mix with the soy sauce and garlic in a bowl.
2. To make the batter, mix the flour and paprika on a rimmed plate or in a wide bowl and season well with salt and pepper. In a separate small bowl, mix the buttermilk and cider vinegar. Dip a tofu cube into the flour mixture, then into the buttermilk mixture and then again into the flour mixture. Place on a baking tray and repeat with the remaining cubes.
3. Meanwhile, heat the air fryer to 200C. Spray the tofu nuggets with the olive oil spray. Place one layer of tofu nuggets on the rack or in the basket (you may have to do this in two batches) and cook for 6 minutes, then shake and return for another 3–4 minutes. Repeat with the remaining nuggets.
4. Serve warm with sweet chilli sauce, if using.

Notes:
1. For a vegan option, use nut milk with the juice of half a lemon to replace the buttermilk.
2. Use chicken cubes instead of tofu for a fakeaway-style crispy chicken nugget. The cooking time may need to increase by a minute or two so check that the chicken is cooked through before you serve.
3. This recipe was developed using a 5.5 litre/9½ pint air fryer.

Air Fryer Roast Sprouts

Get roasted, golden Brussels sprouts in the air fryer in minutes with this festive recipe. With pancetta and chestnuts, it's the perfect side dish without needing to fire up the oven.

Servings: 4   **Cooking Time:** 10 to 30 Mins.

Ingredients:

- 500g/1lb 2oz small Brussels sprouts, peeled and halved
- 180g/6¼oz ready-to-eat chestnuts, halved
- 1 tbsp olive oil
- 100g/3½oz pancetta cubes
- salt and freshly ground black pepper

Directions:

1. Preheat the air fryer to 180C. Toss the sprouts and chestnuts with the oil in a bowl. Season well with salt and pepper and then stir in the pancetta.
2. Add the sprout mixture to the air fryer in a single layer – you may need to do this in batches. Cook for 18–20 minutes, turning halfway through, until the sprouts are tender on the inside and crisp on the outside and the pancetta is crisp.

Mini Hasselback Potatoes

These little hasselback canapés can be made in an air fryer or the oven. They take a little effort to get them to open up and crisp nicely, but it's worth it. Just make sure you don't overcrowd the fryer, and turn them regularly so they don't get stuck together.

Servings: 6-8   Cooking Time: 10 to 30 Mins.

Ingredients:

- 800g/1lb 2oz baby new potatoes
- 3 tbsp vegetable oil
- 2 tsp flaky sea salt
- For the sour cream and chive dip
- 100g/3½oz soured cream
- 2 tbsp chopped chives
- salt and freshly ground black pepper

Directions:

1. Fill a large bowl with water. Put each potato on the chopping board between two chopsticks (or two wooden spoon handles). Using a sharp knife, slice the potato partway through, creating 1mm "leaves" (the chopsticks will prevent you from cutting all the way through).

2. Put the sliced potatoes into the bowl of water to soak while you slice the remaining potatoes. Give the potatoes a little wash, squeezing the ends to open the "leaves" up to get the water in between each slice. Any starch between the slices tends to stick them back together as they cook.

3. Drain the potatoes and roll them onto a clean tea towel to dry them as much as possible. Dry the bowl, then return the potatoes to the bowl and drizzle over the oil, ideally getting it in between the slices. Rub the potatoes all over with the oil so they are coated.

4. Sprinkle each potato with a pinch of flaky salt, trying to get it between the potato slices.

5. Preheat the air fryer to 180C (or an oven to 200C/180C Fan/Gas 6). Cook the potatoes in the air fryer for 25–30 minutes, shaking every 10 minutes if the machine doesn't have a turning paddle, until the potatoes are cooked through and the slices are crisped up. They should be golden brown and the "leaves" will be crisp. (If baking, cook the potatoes for 30–40 minutes.)

Notes:

1. Serve these salty snacks just as they come, or grate over some Parmesan before serving. You can easily double the recipe. If you're making them in the oven they'll take the same amount of time, but you may need to air fry in two batches.

Teriyaki Root Vegetable Salad With Crispy Tofu

Servings: 2   **Cooking Time:** 10 to 30 Mins.

Ingredients:

- For the teriyaki dressing
- 60ml/2¼fl oz dark soy sauce
- 2 tbsp honey
- 1 tbsp sesame oil
- 1 tbsp rice vinegar or white wine vinegar
- 1 tsp cornflour
- 2 garlic cloves, crushed
- For the salad
- 200g/7oz firm tofu, cut into 2cm/¾in cubes and patted dry with kitchen paper
- 1 tbsp olive oil
- 1 tbsp cornflour
- 300g/10½oz celeriac, julienned
- 2 carrots, julienned
- 1 parsnip, julienned
- 100g/3½oz kale, stems removed and leaves torn
- pinch sesame seeds
- salt

Directions:

1. Preheat the oven to 200C/180C Fan/Gas 6 and put a baking tray on the middle shelf to heat up. (Or see Recipe Tip for air fryer instructions)
2. To make the dressing, whisk all of the ingredients together in a small saucepan, then bring to the boil. Cook for 2 minutes until thick and glossy, then remove from the heat and leave to cool.
3. Put the tofu in a large bowl, add 1 tablespoon of the dressing and drizzle over the olive oil. Stir to coat. Sprinkle over the cornflour, stir again, then tip onto the preheated baking tray. Roast for 25 minutes, turning halfway through cooking.
4. Meanwhile, tip the vegetables into a large bowl, add a pinch of salt and massage together for a couple of minutes – this helps to soften them, and in turn soak up more dressing. Once the vegetables are soft, pour in 3–4 tablespoons of the dressing and toss to coat.
5. Divide the salad between 2 serving bowls, top with the crispy tofu and sprinkle over the sesame seeds.

Notes:

1. Use a julienne peeler to shred the vegetables. They are relatively cheap and make prepping salads like this really easy. If you don't have one you can grate the vegetables.
2. Plan ahead and prepare the tofu the night before. Cut into cubes, pat dry, then sandwich between a few sheets of kitchen paper. Weigh down with a plate on top and chill overnight. The more moisture you can remove in advance, the crispier the tofu will be.
3. You can cook the tofu in an air fryer. Just coat in cornflour then drizzle or spray with oil and air fry for 10 minutes at 180C.
4. Any leftover dressing will keep for up to a week in an airtight container in the fridge.

Baked Vegetable Crisps

These vegetable crisps make a colourful snack. Try mixing up the veg and seasonings – swap purple beetroot for golden ones, carrots for sweet potatoes or parsnip for celeriac. Our method is oven baked – see our recipe tip below for an air fryer version.

Servings: 3-4   Cooking Time: 10 to 30 Mins.

Ingredients:

- 2 beetroot, scrubbed and very thinly sliced on a mandolin or with a vegetable peeler
- 2 carrots, scrubbed and very thinly sliced on a mandolin or with a vegetable peeler
- 1 large parsnip, scrubbed and very thinly sliced on a mandolin or with a vegetable peeler
- 1 tbsp light rapeseed, vegetable or sunflower oil
- ½ tsp dried oregano or herbes de Provence (optional)
- ¼ tsp garlic granules or powder (optional)
- salt and freshly ground black pepper

Directions:

1. Lay the vegetables on a tray and pat dry using kitchen paper or a clean tea towel. If you have time, leave them sandwiched in kitchen paper for 5–10 minutes to really dry out – this will give a crisper result.
2. Preheat the oven to 190C/170C Fan/Gas 5.
3. Put the vegetables in a big bowl, drizzle over the oil and some salt and pepper and mix with your hands, working the oil through thoroughly until all the vegetables are coated. Spread the vegetables evenly on two baking trays. Bake for 15 minutes, then turn over and bake for a further 8–12 minutes until dried out and golden brown.
4. Scatter with the herbs and spices, if using, and leave to cool and crisp up before serving.

Notes:

1. These are best eaten on the day you make them, but you can store them in an airtight container for up to 3 days. To serve, put them into a hot oven for about 3 minutes to crisp up. After this second baking they should stay crisp for the rest of their shelf life.
2. To air-fry, follow step 1, then mix the veg slices and peelings with the oil, salt and pepper. Air-fry in small batches at 180C for 5–7 minutes or until dry and browning. The parsnip and smaller beetroot crisps might be done first. Leave to crisp up on trays or plates while you cook the rest. When all the crisps are done, mix together the herbs and spices, scatter over and gently stir to coat.
3. To avoid food waste, you can make crisps from any kind of potato or root veg peelings. Season and oil as above, then cook for 12–15 minutes in a preheated oven at 190C/170C Fan/Gas 5, turning halfway, or 8–10 minutes in an air fryer at 180C.

Curried Pumpkin Soup

Servings: 4 **Cooking Time:** 1 to 2 Hours

Ingredients:

- 1kg/2lb 4oz pumpkin, peeled, seeds removed and flesh cut into 7cm/2¾in chunks
- 3–4 tbsp olive oil
- 1 tsp salt, plus extra if desired
- 1 tsp chilli powder
- 1 tsp ground coriander
- 1 tsp ground cumin
- 1 onion, roughly chopped
- 3 tomatoes, cut into quarters
- 6–8 garlic cloves, flattened and peeled
- 400ml tin coconut milk
- freshly ground black pepper
- For the tarka
- 4 tbsp vegetable oil
- 1 tsp cumin seeds
- 1 tsp black mustard seeds
- 4–6 garlic cloves, thinly sliced
- 1–3 green jalapeño chillies, thinly sliced

Directions:

1. Preheat the oven to 180C/160C Fan/Gas 4. Rub the pumpkin with the oil and sprinkle with the salt, chilli powder, ground coriander and ground cumin.
2. Add to a large roasting tin along with the onion, tomatoes and garlic. Roast for 1-1½ hours, turning every 30 minutes to make sure everything is soft and caramelised (pumpkins vary hugely in how long they need to be cooked for, the more water they contain the longer they will take).
3. Once the vegetables are tender, tip everything from the roasting tin into a food processor and blend with the coconut milk until smooth. Pour into a large saucepan or casserole and keep warm. Season with salt and pepper. Add a splash of water if needed to thin the soup.
4. To make the tarka, heat the oil in the smallest saucepan you have and add the cumin seeds. Once they start to pop, add the black mustard seeds, garlic and chillies. Cook for 1 minute until the garlic is just lightly browned then take off the heat. Immediately spoon the tarka over the soup and cover with a lid. Leave for 5 minutes before mixing the tarka into the soup and serving.

Notes:

1. If you have a high-powered food processor, and if the skin of the pumpkin is thin enough, skip peeling the pumpkin and roast with the skin on. Crown Prince squashes (the pale blue-grey pumpkins) or an acorn squash have very thick skins and are difficult to peel.
2. As an alternative, halve the squash, scoop out the seeds and stringy centre, and roast the halves, cut-side down, as in the recipe. Carefully scoop the cooked flesh out from the skin with a spoon and blend as in the recipe.
3. You can also roast the vegetables in an air-fryer at 180C for 10–15 minutes. Leave the garlic cloves unpeeled and the tomatoes whole. Shake the vegetables every 5 minutes so that they cook evenly. You may need to halve the recipe depending on the size of your air-fryer.

Vietnamese-Style Loaded Fries

Inspired by Vietnam's famous banh mi sandwich, a popular street food with hot, spicy and sweet flavours, these fries are loaded with sweet glazed tofu, quick pickled vegetables, mayonnaise and hot sauce. If you have an air fryer, you can use it to cook the fries.

Servings: 2   Cooking Time: 10 to 30 Mins.

Ingredients:

- 500g/1lb 2oz frozen French fries
- For the quick pickled vegetables
- 4 tbsp rice wine vinegar
- ½ tsp sea salt
- ½ tsp golden caster sugar
- 1 large carrot, peeled and cut into thin matchsticks
- 4–6 radishes, thinly sliced
- For the glazed tofu
- 2 tbsp soy sauce
- 1 tsp lemongrass paste
- 1 tsp soft light brown sugar
- 1 lime, juice only
- 280g/10oz extra firm tofu, drained
- ½ tbsp light oil
- small handful fresh coriander leaves, to garnish
- Japanese mayonnaise, to serve
- sriracha chilli sauce, to serve

Directions:

1. Cook the French fries according to packet instructions, or for 20 minutes on the chip setting (this should be roughly 200C) in an air fryer.
2. Meanwhile, make the quick pickles. In a small bowl, stir the vinegar, salt and caster sugar together until dissolved. Add the vegetables, stir to coat in the pickling liquid and set aside.
3. To make the sauce for the glazed tofu, whisk together the soy sauce, lemongrass paste, brown sugar and lime juice in a small bowl. Set aside.
4. Squeeze as much excess moisture as possible out of the tofu and pat dry on kitchen paper. Cut into bite-sized cubes.
5. Heat the oil in a large frying pan over a medium–high heat until shimmering. Add the tofu and fry for about 15 minutes, turning occasionally. The tofu cubes should become slightly browned and crisped around the edges.
6. Turn the heat up to high and add the sauce. Leave the sauce to bubble away, stirring occasionally, until it has reduced to a sticky glaze that coats the tofu cubes.
7. Divide the cooked French fries between two bowls and divide the tofu pieces between them. Pat the quick pickles dry on kitchen paper and sprinkle them over the bowls along with the coriander leaves. Drizzle each bowl generously with Japanese mayonnaise and sriracha sauce before serving.

Notes:

1. Japanese mayonnaise is richer and creamier than European-style mayo; it is made with rice vinegar and is usually sold in a squeezy bottle. If you can't find it, you can use regular mayo instead.

Easy Onion Rings

A pub-style side, or serve as a starter or nibble with ketchup, light soured cream or a spicy dipping sauce such as sriracha or American-style mustard. These can be baked in the oven or made in an air fryer – either way they're healthier than traditional deep-fried onion rings.

Servings: 2   **Cooking Time: 10 to 30 Mins.**

Ingredients:

- 1 large onion, sliced into rings about 1.5cm/⅝in thick
- 4 tbsp plain flour
- 1 free-range egg
- 1 tbsp milk (dairy or unsweetened non-dairy)
- 60g/2¼oz panko breadcrumbs
- cooking oil spray
- salt and freshly ground black pepper

Directions:

1. Preheat the oven to 200C/180C Fan/Gas 6, or the air fryer to 180C.
2. Carefully separate the onion slices into rings; some rings should be one onion-layer thick, others two layers.
3. Put half the flour in a shallow bowl and season with salt and pepper. Put the remaining flour in another shallow bowl and whisk in the egg and milk to make a smooth batter. Put the panko breadcrumbs in another shallow bowl.
4. Dip the onion rings into the seasoned flour, making sure they are thoroughly coated all over. Lightly tap off excess flour. Put the floured rings into the batter and flip a few times to coat completely, shaking off excess batter. Finally add them to the breadcrumbs and press crumbs all over them.
5. Spray a baking sheet or the inside of your air fryer with cooking oil. Add the onion rings in a single layer – if air frying you'll need to do them in batches. Spray the tops of the onion rings with more oil.
6. Bake in the oven for 18–20 minutes, turning after 8–10 minutes. Air-fry for 10 minutes, turning halfway through. Keep the first batches of air fryer onion rings warm in a low oven while you cook the rest, then serve immediately.

Air Fryer Yoghurt Custard Toast

Servings: 2 **Cooking Time: 10 Mins.**

Ingredients:
- 2 slices brioche
- 1 free-range egg, at room temperature
- 3 tbsp plain yoghurt
- 3 tsp runny honey or maple syrup
- 75g/2¾oz fresh or frozen raspberries or other soft fruit

Directions:
1. Preheat the air fryer to 175C. Using the back of a spoon, flatten down the centre of the brioche slices to leave a border around the edge.
2. Beat together the egg, yoghurt and 2 teaspoons honey in a small bowl. Spoon the custard into the wells in the brioche and then arrange the fruit on top.
3. Air-fry for 7–8 minutes until the custard has set and the bread is crisp. Drizzle over the remaining honey and serve warm.

Notes:
1. If your air fryer has a deep drawer, lay the bread on a piece of baking paper to make lifting the toast in and out easier.
2. If you don't have an air fryer you can cook these yoghurt custard toasts in the oven preheated to 200C/180C Fan/Gas 6 for 15 minutes.

Air Fryer Apple-Topped Cake

This low-maintenance air fryer cake is really easy and quick to make. It bakes perfectly in an air fryer and the apples on top keep it lovely and moist.

Servings: 8 **Cooking Time: 30 Mins. to 1 Hour**

Ingredients:

- 150g/5½oz unsalted butter, softened
- 150g/5½oz caster sugar
- 200g/7oz self-raising flour
- 2 large free-range eggs
- 2 tbsp milk (full-fat or skimmed)
- 2 small red apples, cored, cut in half and finely sliced into half moons
- 2 tsp light brown sugar
- icing sugar, for dusting
- double cream, to serve (optional)

Directions:

1. Line a 20cm/8in round cake tin (or a cake tin that will fit inside the air fryer) with greaseproof paper.
2. Whisk the butter, caster sugar, flour, eggs and milk in a large bowl using an electric whisk or in a stand mixer. Mix on a medium speed for a few minutes until well combined. Heat the air fryer to 160C.
3. Pour the batter into the tin and arrange the apple slices on top in concentric circles. Sprinkle over the brown sugar to finish.
4. Bake for 30 minutes (use the dessert or cake setting if there is one). Then reduce the temperature to 150C and bake for a further 5–6 minutes, or until cooked through. (These timings work for a 20cm/8in cake tin – if using a smaller tin, you may need to adjust the timings. Start with 5 minutes more baking time and then test to see if it is done. See Recipe Tip.)
5. Remove from the air fryer, leave to cool for a few minutes and then remove the cake from the tin. Allow to cool then dust with the icing sugar. Slice and serve with the cream, if using.

Notes:

1. Substitutions
2. Replace 50g/1¾oz flour with 50g/1¾oz ground almonds for a delicious nutty twist, replace the sliced apples with sliced plums, or add 50g/1¾oz chopped pistachios to the cake base.
3. Timings
4. This recipe suits a 20cm/8in cake tin. If using a smaller tin, bear in mind that the cooking time may increase. It is best to adjust the timings as detailed in the recipe and check every 3–4 minutes. If you do need to increase the cooking time, you may want to cover the top of the cake loosely with foil if it is getting a little too dark.
5. This cake is best served on the day it is made, but it can also be tightly covered with cling film and frozen for up to 1 month. Defrost completely before serving.
6. This recipe was developed using a 5.5 litre/9½ pint air fryer.

4-Ingredient Air Fryer Cookies

These 4-ingredient air fryer cookies couldn't be easier to make. All you need is some chocolate hazelnut spread, milk, flour and some white chocolate to drizzle.

Servings: 6   **Cooking Time: 10 Mins.**

Ingredients:
- 100g/3½oz hazelnut chocolate spread
- 75g/2¾oz plain flour
- 3 tbsp full-fat milk
- 40g/1½oz chocolate (any type), melted, to decorate

Directions:
1. Preheat the air fryer to 180C. Place the chocolate spread, flour and milk in a bowl. Mix well and then, using your hands, bring together to make a firm dough.
2. Roll the mixture into 6 evenly sized balls then flatten into cookies. Lay a sheet of baking paper in the air fryer basket then place the cookies on top, leaving a little space between each one.
3. Air fry for 8–10 minutes then carefully lift out. Drizzle over the melted chocolate and leave to cool before serving.

Notes:
1. If you don't have an air fryer, you can cook these in an oven preheated to 200C/180C Fan/Gas 6 for 12–14 minutes.
2. You may find the mixture easier to roll if you chill the hazelnut chocolate spread before using. You could also chill the dough in the fridge before baking.
3. Use plain chocolate spread if you like and decorate them anyway you want to.

Air Fryer Courgette, Almond And Pine Nut Cake

Courgettes, ground almonds, pine nuts, lemon and sultanas combine in this deliciously moist Tuscan cake, easily made in the air fryer.

Servings: 8-10   Cooking Time: 1 to 2 Hours

Ingredients:

- 150g/5½oz unsalted butter, plus extra for greasing
- 150g/5½oz brown sugar
- 3 free-range eggs
- 30g/1oz plain flour
- 1 tsp baking powder
- pinch salt
- 200g/7oz ground almonds
- 200g/7oz courgettes, grated
- 150g/5½oz sultanas
- 70g/2½oz pine nuts
- 1 lemon, grated zest and juice
- icing sugar, for dusting

Directions:

1. Preheat the air fryer to 170C. Set to the bake setting if your air fryer has this.
2. Grease a 18cm/7in round cake tin and line the base with greaseproof paper.
3. Cream the butter and sugar together until pale, then beat in the eggs, one at a time, until all are incorporated.
4. Gently fold through the flour, baking powder, salt and the ground almonds.
5. Add the courgettes, sultanas, 50g/1¾oz of the pine nuts, the lemon zest and juice.
6. Spoon the mixture into the cake tin and scatter over the remaining pine nuts. Cook in the air fryer for 25 minutes.
7. Cover with kitchen foil and cook for a further 35–40 minutes, until cooked through. Test by inserting a skewer into the centre of the cake: it should come out clean. If not, cook it for a little longer.
8. Leave to cool in the tin for 10 minutes, then turn out onto a wire rack and leave to cool completely.
9. To serve, dust with icing sugar.

Notes:

1. Cooking time can vary, depending on the air fryer.
2. If you have time, soak the sultanas in lemon juice to make them plump and juicy before you add them to the cake mixture.
3. The smaller the courgettes, the sweeter they are.
4. Try this with carrots instead of courgettes.
5. The cake needs to cool completely before slicing.

Air Fryer Peach Turnovers

Use your air fryer to make these peach turnovers, fragrant with dates, orange and rosemary. They're a great little treat for any occasion, from breakfast to afternoon tea, a summer dinner or a picnic.

Servings: 4   Cooking Time: 10 to 30 Mins.

Ingredients:

- 4 ripe peaches, stones removed, roughly chopped
- 4 dates, stones removed, roughly chopped
- 1 sprig fresh rosemary, leaves finely chopped
- 2 tbsp caster sugar
- 1 orange, grated zest and juice
- plain flour, for dusting
- 500g block readymade puff pastry
- 1 free-range egg, beaten
- For the topping
- 4 tbsp icing sugar
- ½ tsp finely chopped fresh rosemary leaves
- ½ orange, juice only
- 2 tbsp toasted almonds

Directions:

1. Put the peaches, dates, rosemary, a tablespoon of caster sugar, the orange juice and half the zest into a heatproof dish that fits into your air fryer.
2. Air-fry for 10 minutes, stirring a couple of times, until the peaches just start to break down. Set aside to cool.
3. Preheat the air fryer to 180C.
4. Once the filling is cool, lightly dust a work surface with flour. Roll out the puff pastry to make a square roughly 34x34cm/13½x13½in. Cut this into four smaller squares.
5. Spoon a quarter of the peach filling into the corner of each square. Brush the edges with beaten egg, then bring one corner over to meet the other, creating a triangle shape and covering the filling. Use a fork to press down and seal the edges.
6. Brush each turnover with beaten egg and sprinkle over the remaining caster sugar.
7. Air-fry for 10 minutes, then flip over and cook for a further 5 minutes.
8. While the turnovers are cooking, make the topping. Mix together the icing sugar, rosemary and about 2 teaspoons of the orange juice to make a thick smooth paste that you can drizzle.
9. Once the turnovers have cooled slightly, use a spoon or piping bag to drizzle the topping over in thin lines. Scatter over the toasted almonds and serve.

Notes:

1. The filling can be made in advance and kept in the fridge.
2. If you are short of time you can pop the filling into the freezer for 15 minutes to chill down faster.
3. If your air fryer is small, you may need to cook the turnovers in batches; pop the uncooked turnovers into the fridge until they are ready to cook.

Roasted Pumpkin Seeds

Make the most of your Halloween pumpkin and roast the seeds for a healthy snack among all the treats.

Servings: 4-6   Cooking Time: 10 to 30 Mins.

Ingredients:
- 1 large jack o' lantern pumpkin, or other pumpkin or squash
- 1 tbsp vegetable oil
- ½ tsp salt or 1–2 tsp of your favourite seasoning mix, such as Cajun, BBQ or fajita

Directions:
1. With a small, sharp knife, cut the top off the pumpkin and use a large spoon to scrape out the stringy pith and seeds into a bowl. Separate the seeds from the pith as best you can and put the seeds into a sieve or colander, removing as much pith as you can. Discard the pith.
2. Preheat the oven to 200C/180C Fan/Gas 6.
3. Rinse the seeds well, picking off any bits of pith and pumpkin flesh. (The pumpkin tends to stick to your hands, so a good technique for cleaning the seeds is to run your hands through the seeds and rinse them clean of pumpkin bits a couple of times.) Drain well, then spread out on a clean tea towel and pat dry.
4. Transfer the seeds to a large baking tray (or use two, so that the seeds are well spread out) and drizzle them with oil. Sprinkle with salt or seasoning mix and give them a good stir so that they are all coated.
5. Roast in the oven for 15–20 minutes, stirring them halfway through, until the seeds are toasted and golden brown. Leave to cool on the tray, then pour into a bowl to serve. They will crisp up as they cool, so don't try to eat them too soon!

Notes:
1. You can make this at any time of year, using the seeds from any type of pumpkin or squash.
2. The roasted seeds will keep for a day or so in an airtight container, but they tend to become chewy over time.
3. To make pumpkin seeds in the air fryer, preheat the machine to 180C. Add the unoiled pumpkin seeds to the basket and cook for 1 minute to dry them. Tip them into a bowl and coat with oil, salt and spices (if using). Return them to the basket and cook for a further 3-4 minutes or until golden-brown. Tip onto a plate and allow to cool and crisp up before eating.

Air Fryer Apple, Pear And Raspberry Crumble

Versatile, quick and easy, crumble is always popular. Here's how to make it in the air fryer. This version uses apples, pears and raspberries, but use whatever fruit is in season.

Servings: 4 **Cooking Time:** 10 to 30 Mins.

Ingredients:

- 3 Bramley apples, peeled, cored and roughly chopped
- 2 ripe pears, peeled, cored and sliced
- 4 bay leaves, lightly crushed
- 1 tbsp brown sugar
- 1 orange, grated zest and juice
- 150g/5½oz fresh raspberries
- For the topping
- 40g/1½oz rolled oats
- 60g/2¼oz plain flour
- 60g/2¼oz ground almonds
- 60g/2¼oz butter, cubed
- pinch sea salt
- 6 amaretti biscuits, finely crushed
- 40g/1½oz soft brown sugar

Directions:

1. Preheat the air fryer to 180C.
2. Put the apples, pears, bay leaves, sugar, orange zest and juice into a heatproof dish that fits into your air fryer, about 18cm/7in in diameter. Mix together, then air-fry for 15 minutes, stirring a couple of times during cooking.
3. Remove and discard the bay leaves and stir through the raspberries.
4. To make the topping, put the oats, flour, ground almonds and butter into a bowl with a pinch of sea salt and rub together to incorporate the butter. Stir through the amaretti crumbs and sugar, then sprinkle this mixture over the fruit.
5. Cook in the air fryer for 10 minutes. Serve with a dollop of crème fraîche, ice cream or custard.

Notes:

1. I like the filling of a crumble to be quite tart as the topping is very sweet, but if you have a sweet tooth, you can add a little more sugar to the fruit mix.
2. Both the fruit filling and the topping can be made in advance and frozen.

Homemade Granola

Nutty, fruity wholesome goodness is what homemade granola is all about. Please feel free to ad lib here, with substitutions such as honey for maple syrup, raisins, apricots or dried apples for the dried cranberries and cashews for the whole almonds.

Servings: 3   Cooking Time: 10 to 30 Mins.

Ingredients:

- 125ml/4fl oz maple syrup (or honey or golden syrup)
- 25g/1oz caster sugar
- 25ml/1fl oz sunflower oil
- ½ tsp vanilla extract
- 500g/1lb 2oz jumbo rolled oats
- 175g/6oz mixed seeds (like pumpkin, sunflower, sesame or linseeds)
- 150g/5oz pecans (or walnuts)
- 50g/2oz whole almonds
- 25g/1oz flaked almonds
- 75g/2¾oz desiccated coconut
- pinch of salt (optional)
- 2 tsp cinnamon (optional)
- 150g/5½oz dried cranberries (or raisins, dates or other dried fruit)

Directions:

1. Preheat the oven to 170C/325F/Gas 3. Line two large roasting trays with parchment paper and set aside.
2. Put the maple syrup, sugar, oil and vanilla extract into a large bowl and mix well. Then toss in the oats, mixed seeds, pecans (or walnuts), whole almonds, flaked almonds, coconut and salt and cinnamon (if using). Give it a good stir and then get your hands in, picking it up and letting it fall down to coat and moisten everything really well.
3. Pour the mixture onto the roasting trays and spread it out evenly. Bake in the oven for about 15 minutes, giving it a good stir and swapping them about on their shelves half way through.
4. The granola should be golden-brown when cooked. Remove and leave to cool completely before stirring the cranberries through. Store in an airtight container for up to a month.

Notes:

1. You can make this granola in the air-fryer, though we recommend you start with a half batch. Mix as above. Line a basket air-fryer with foil, or use a baking tray - depending on what style air-fryer you own. bake at 170(for 15 minutes, stirring the granola every 5 minutes.